STORY SMART

STORY SMART

Using the Science of Story to Persuade, Influence, Inspire, and Teach

KENDALL HAVEN

 LIBRARIES UNLIMITED

AN IMPRINT OF ABC-CLIO, LLC
Santa Barbara, California • Denver, Colorado • Oxford, England

Library of Congress Cataloging-in-Publication Data

Haven, Kendall F.
　　Story smart : using the science of story to persuade, influence, inspire, and teach / Kendall Haven.
　　　　pages cm.
　　Includes bibliographical references and index.
　　ISBN 978–1–61069–811–5 (pbk.) — ISBN 978–1–61069–812–2 (ebook)　1.　Storytelling—Psychological aspects.　I. Title.
LB1042.H3886　2014
372.67′7—dc23　　　　　　　2014023483

ISBN: 978–1–61069–811–5
EISBN: 978–1–61069–812–2

18　17　16　15　14　　　1　2　3　4　5

This book is also available on the World Wide Web as an eBook.
Visit www.abc-clio.com for details.

Libraries Unlimited
An Imprint of ABC-CLIO, LLC

ABC-CLIO, LLC
130 Cremona Drive, P.O. Box 1911
Santa Barbara, California 93116-1911

This book is printed on acid-free paper ∞

Manufactured in the United States of America

This book is dedicated to Roni Berg,
the love of my life.
Far more than as a talented and thoughtful editor,
for *this* book, she has felt more like my co-author.
You will feel—and benefit from—her guiding fingerprint
on every page.

CONTENTS

PART I

HOOKED ON STORY

TALK STORY

Storytelling has become the business, science, and brand marketing communications *nom du jour*. Periodicals and journals from *Forbes* to *Business Week* to *Parent* to *Discover* and to *Science* are peppered with recent articles touting the value, power, and effectiveness of storytelling. Suddenly everyone is a storyteller.

For well over 100,000 years before there was writing, humans relied on stories to communicate and to archive (in human memory) all key events, histories, concepts, beliefs, and attitudes. Extensive research has shown that, because of this eons-long dependence on story, human brains are literally evolutionarily hardwired to make sense, to think, to understand, and to remember in specific story terms and elements. The recent research I want to share with you in this book has identified those terms and elements and the neural pathways and processes by which our brains (including every brain in your target audiences) use them. It is not that we *can* use story thinking. It is that our brains are wired so that we *must* use story thinking—all the time.

According to the current common wisdom as expressed in popular journals, storytelling changes lives. Storytelling alters beliefs, values, and behaviors. It exerts powerful influence.

Actually, only a tiny fraction of all of the "stories" we hear or read accomplish that Herculean feat.

Depending on whose research you use, between 98 percent and 99 percent of all of the "stories" you hear/read have no effect on you. They are not vividly imagined in your mind. They do not engage you on a deep emotional level. They are not remembered. They don't change your beliefs, attitudes, or behavior. You don't learn from them.

Question: Why do only those *few* affect us? Why not the rest? How *do* stories persuade, teach, inspire, and exert influence (changing someone's beliefs, attitudes, values, and behavior)? When they don't, *why* don't they? What's in the structure of a story that creates those changes in the receiver's brain and mind?

What do neural and cognitive science research findings (from repeated lab tests to neural scans) say that the words "story" and "storytelling" really mean and refer to? Is there practical information that has emerged from this scientific research to allow people to control and apply that incredible story power?

This book will lay out the hard science research from over a dozen fields of scientific research behind the startling power of story that answers each of those questions. It's all about mastering a specific set of concepts from the amazing world of the science of story to make you and your work . . . *Story Smart*.

■ ■ ■

I WAS WORKING IN THE LAB LATE ONE NIGHT ...

We begin with the first true scientific experiment into the structure of a story ever conducted in a modern EEG lab. This experiment stretched from May 2012 to June 2013.

Each member of each test audience was wired to a 24-channel EEG system, was fitted with cardio and skin galvanic monitors, and had saliva swabs collected both before and after the story to measure oxytocin and dopamine levels. They looked like guinea pigs in a Mel Brooks version of Frankenstein. Video cameras recorded each person's reactions and movement throughout the story. After hearing the story, each subject filled out a written follow-on questionnaire about the story and its characters, and took part in a short oral interview.

I was able to present slightly different versions of the same story to each test audience. (Change character motive for one audience. Change the way I characterize one of the major characters for another. Change the ending point for other audiences.) I was able to test dozens of versions of the same story, varying only a few key sentences from the base version for each group.

This testing let me answer the question: What effect does it create in an audience if I change *this* one part of the story? Or *that* one part? Or these three parts in combination? It allowed me to examine the effect of a story (element by element) in a controlled and replicable way. I would be able to literally watch which changes created strong shifts in physical and neural reaction, and which did not. I would be able to identify those elements/aspects of story that drive personal involvement and strong reaction, and which do not.

I held a great mass of data that linked specific story elements to real-time audience response and to their recorded brain activity. Those EEG charts let us search for known markers of engagement, empathy, character identity, transportation (being transported into the story), and—especially—emotional response. The questionnaire responses and interview discussions allowed me to quantify the audience perception of characters and story (and the shifts in those responses) and tie them back to the specific story shifts I had made for each individual audience.

No one had ever conducted this kind of detailed story assessment before. Did I find what I was looking for? You bet I did!

Truly amazing and profound findings jumped out of that research that every reader of this book can use.

But first we need to step back a bit, lay down a foundation from previous science discoveries, and check your Story IQ.

■ ■ ■

WHAT'S YOUR STORY IQ?

Let's test your Story IQ. Which of the following do you think involve a story?

- *Uncle Fred perches on a kitchen chair doing his impersonation of the president while he makes up silly policy initiatives.*
- *Your grandmother quietly tells you about eight generations worth of family history as she knits.*
- *You tell your spouse about your day.*
- *You tell a joke.*
- *You read an article in* Time *or* Discover *magazine.*
- *You read a stock report or a computer program instruction book.*
- *You read an essay your neighbor wants to submit to the Letters to the Editor section of the local paper.*
- *You read a recipe for venison stew.*
- *You read a short story in a collection of classic literature.*

Are they *all* examples of stories? Are none of them? What makes one a story and another not? Not as clear-cut as you thought it might be, is it? Which involve a "real" story? Which represent an example of a *good* story, an effective story?

If you're looking for definitive answers, I have to disappoint you. The answer for each of those situations is: Maybe yes, maybe no. They each *could* be. The real answer is that I asked the wrong question. The right question would be: What would make each of these into an effective story? That answer would give you some useful information. It is a question I'll answer shortly.

■ ■ ■

EXTRA . . . EXTRA!
READ ALL ABOUT IT!

Let me lay out a few headlines I'll develop and support in this book.

- Your brain is evolutionarily hardwired to think, to understand, to remember, and to recall in specific story terms. More importantly (for you), so is the brain of every person to whom you ever need to communicate. It's not that we *can* use story thinking. It's that we *MUST*. We automatically do. We can't *not* do it.
- Your brain is programmed to make sense of incoming information and experiences in specific story terms. If we can't make it make sense in story terms, we either change the information around so that it *does* make sense or we ignore it.
- Your hardwired Neural Story Net that is responsible for turning incoming information and experiences into story terms in order to make it make sense lies between your sensory organs (eyes and ears) and your conscious brain. You turn *everything* into story form before you pass it to your conscious mind and memory. What reaches your conscious mind is your personalized storied version of what your sensory organs recorded. Everyone in every audience you hope to reach does the same thing to you and your material.
- Research confirms that if you use what I will call effective story structure for your communications, your information reaches a listener's conscious mind and memory more accurately and vividly than if you put that same information into any other narrative form.
- The process of creating effective stories doesn't begin with a story. It *ends* with the story and begins with your messages and with your intended audience.

■ ■ ■

THIS IS A ROLL-UP-YOUR-SLEEVES PRACTICAL GUIDE

This is a how-to book, a practical step-by-step guide to the must-have story-based informational elements that your audiences' story-seeking minds desperately need to find—or to create. I'll anchor that practical guidance on the most recent and advanced neural, cognitive, and psychological science. With that science in hand, you'll be in position to easily harness the incredible power and allure of stories.

Let me be clear about what this book is not. This is not a research report. My previous book, *Story Proof: The Science Behind the Startling Power of Story* (2009), was a research book. For that book I gathered, analyzed, and compared over 150,000 pages of research results from 16 fields of related scientific investigation and used the book to report what I found. True, I have added an additional 200,000 pages of research and have participated in extensive experimentation between that book and this. However, I have designed this book as a "So, what are you supposed to *do* with that information?" book, a practical users guide to harnessing the most powerful and proven form of narrative communication.

You already have a job. And that job is not specifically to tell stories. Yet, each "story" you develop is a powerful tool you can use to better accomplish what you *do* need to get done. This is a straightforward guide to how stories work and to how to use them to better accomplish your personal and organizational goals.

Yes, the information and ideas I present are all backed by extensive lab research (even with stacks of four-color EEG and fMRI printouts) that, in turn, is backed by extensive practical trials with live audiences and actual organizations. But I won't quote from or directly cite most of the now over 1,000 individual references that form the composite mosaic I have used in developing this material over the years. I want to get straight to "What do you need to know to effectively and consistently make successful use of stories?" and to "What are proven, practical steps to using that information?" If you want to get your hands on the references to the research, combine those recent studies I cite here with the greater bulk I listed in *Story Proof*.

Here I want to show you what creates the difference between stories that *do* change beliefs, values, attitudes, knowledge, and behavior . . . and those that head straight for the mental trash basket. I want to share the latest story science—and what that science shows us is truly amazing—and to lay out the core elements and tools of story craft.

■ ■ ■

STORY VERSUS STORY!

A Telling Example	*Between 2003 and 2006, a researcher posed this question to over 1,000 audiences of business executives: A new employee in your company receives an intensive, professionally designed 20-hour orientation. You then turn that new employee loose on the factory floor. As he enters, another employee throws his arm around the new fella's shoulder and says, "Let me tell you a story about how things really work around here" (Cron 2012, p. 18).* *The question was: Would your new employees believe the 20-hour training or the 10-minute story? Without exception, they said, "the story."*

Intuitively, we know that people believe stories, that stories grab and hold human minds. Yet—and this is the key point—virtually none of these same 1,000+ executives said that they had ever considered rewriting their new employee training into the form of stories. Stories were more convincing, more believable, more appealing. They admitted it. They believed it. But they weren't gonna use them!

It should *always* be all about getting results—the results you want and need. Period. You want to do what works; what gets results. Yet, most people consistently sabotage their own stories, unwittingly serving as their own worst enemy and almost guaranteeing that their stories will fail to engage, to hold the attention of, or to influence, teach, inspire, and/or persuade their intended audience. Part of that sabotage comes in the delivery—especially for live, oral presentations. Yet most of it comes from the counterproductive manner in which we naturally tend to form and structure our story-based narrative material. That is what we will solve in this book.

Stories are our age-old guides for being successful humans. As if they are now woven into our DNA, we are cued to resonate to their form and structure. That gives this particular thing we call story incredible power and the ability to exert strong influence. That is where they become powerful tools in your arsenal.

"We use stories to pass on accumulated wisdom, beliefs, and values. Through stories we explain how things are, why they are, and our role and purpose. Stories are the building blocks of knowledge, the foundation of memory and learning. Stories connect us with our humanness and link past, present, and future by teaching us to anticipate the possible consequences of our actions." A quote from the National Storytelling Association Board of Directors definition of Storytelling (8/97).

It would seem that effectively using stories should and would be the most natural thing in the world. Too bad that's not what researchers find.

You use stories for internal organizational purposes with workers, managers, and volunteers. You use stories to improve your ability to teach, inspire, and persuade. You use stories to improve your success with funders, the public, and your customers. You write articles and brochures. You issue press releases. You blog. You give talks, speeches, lectures, and workshops . . . and . . . nothing. No gain; no results. Shockingly, some researchers estimate that as many as a third of the stories issued by nonprofits actually prove to be *counter*productive—worse than doing nothing!

You want your stories to have impact. You want them to be remembered and to change people's attitudes and actions. You want to make people see things from your viewpoint, your perspective, and your beliefs. You want to *influence* them.

Influence is the research term for persuade, convince, inspire, or teach. It means to change someone's beliefs, attitudes, values, knowledge, and/or behavior. While you hold an audience's **attention** (focused mental activity over time), you have the chance to influence them with your information and messages. In order to garner and hold attention, you must **engage** them. Engagement becomes the essential gateway to influence. **Stories** effectively engage and hold attention.

> *If engagement is the essential gateway to influence, then stories are the key that opens that gate.*

Before we get too far along, we need to agree on the usage of a few words that will appear repeatedly in this book. Working definitions for other terms will appear as they become relevant to the discussion.

The first of these words is "*effective*," as in "effective stories."

Effective stories: Stories that 1) successfully engage and hold that engagement and 2) also accomplish the communications *purpose* (your influence or teaching) for which they were created.

As I use it in this book, the term "effective story" holds that dual mandate. If it doesn't successfully deliver your information and messaging accurately and vividly to the conscious mind and memory of your intended audience, it might be a *good* story, but it isn't an effective one.

Audience: Like the proverbial tree that falls in the woods, a story requires an audience if it is to have meaning and purpose. As I use it in this book, an audience is the group that receives a story. It can be readers, listeners, or viewers. When we get to the point of intentionally designing stories to accomplish some purpose, "audience" will be synonymous with "target audience" or "intended audiences."

Storyteller: You are the one who creates the story, writes the story, shares the story, or tells the story. Terms such as "storyteller," "story writer," "story crafter" (or "creator"), and "story performer" all refer to the person who delivers the story to the intended audience.

■ ■ ■

—— EFFECTIVE OR NOT EFFECTIVE...
THAT IS THE QUESTION ——

Do stories have to look like classic once-upon-a-time folk or fairy stories to be effective? Not at all.

A Telling Example	*In 2005, three groups of quantitative MBA's were shown a new ad campaign for a California winery. During the presentation, one group was also told the story of the company's founder and of his father, a wine maker from Europe. The second group was shown the campaign plus various tables of statistics about sales projections, market shares, etc. The third group was shown just the ad campaign (Cron 2012, p. 91).* *Each group was asked questions to determine if they believed the winery's policy statements in the ad campaign. The only group that believed the ad campaign and said that it would be believed by the public was the group who heard the story. Story creates believability—even for skeptical, quantitatively trained MBAs.* *The winery folk never said, "Here's the story of the company founder ..." They simply wove that key story information into their pitch. That is as effective a use of story as is launching into a "Once upon a time ..." tale. "Story" is a way of thinking about your communication combined with the conscious use of a set of specific tools in order to control and direct how your communications are received, heard, and internalized by your listeners/readers.*

Effective story use is as much a way of thinking, approaching, and planning as it is the formatted layout or the fixed template of a physical thing: "the story." Understand the science behind the power of story (Part II) and the specific elements that characterize effective story structure (Part III), and you'll be in position to customize that power to your specific purposes and needs. In Part IV you'll learn the very latest research that peels back the veil that has always shrouded story influence in mystery. Finally, in Part V we'll walk through the process of converting your themes and messages into the form of effective stories.

Neuroscientist Anthony Damasio (2010, p. 293) said, "Storytelling is something brains automatically do, naturally and implicitly ... It should be no surprise that stories pervade the entire fabric of human societies and cultures."

Lisa Cron (2012, p. 9) wrote, "Neuroscientists believe the reason our already overloaded brain devotes so much precious time, energy, and space to allowing us to get lost in a story is that without stories, we'd be toast. Stories allow us to simulate intense experience without having to actually live through them. Stories allow us to experience the world before we have to actually experience it."

In the words of famed cognitive scientist Steven Pinker (1997, p. 543), "Stories supply us with a mental catalogue of the fatal conundrums we might face someday and the outcomes of strategies we could deploy in them. Because we need that vicarious experience, our brains are wired to think in stories."

Extracting from the chapters on brain physiology and function in V. S. Ramachandran's respected 2004 book, neural scientists can tell us that embedded in the front part of the temporal lobe lies the hippocampus (concerned with memory). The limbic system, including the amygdala, mediates emotional arousal. Just below the occipital lobe lies the cerebellum, which is concerned mainly with timing and movements. The fusiform gyrus—concerned with processing faces—sits on the inner side of the temporal lobe and sends signals to the amygdala ... etcetera, etcetera.

But so what? Your mission is to persuade, to inspire, to influence, to teach. You don't care where in the brain a response happens—as long as it *does* happen. Let mid-line theta shifts create a mu suppression that triggers an empathetic-like signal in the amygdala. You really don't care if the hypothalamus has to perform a handstand while juggling for the lateral cortex in order to generate an empathetic response. You just need to know that what you do with you material—your story—will result in that empathetic magic trick being performed. Still, once someone dives into the human brain to discover the science of how and why humans perceive, understand, interpret, and make sense as they do, we can all take advantage of that science to advance our ability to use story form and structure more effectively and consistently.

Rose (2011, p. 73) wrote, "Just as the brain detects patterns in the visual forms of nature and in sound, so, too, it detects patterns in information. Stories are recognizable patterns, and in those patterns we find meaning. We use stories to make sense of the world and to share that understanding with others. They are the signal within the noise." This book will give you mastery over the elements of that "signal."

Here are a couple of additional quotes from another research-based author (Gottschall 2012, p. 8) to help set the stage for the central themes of this book. "Story's role in human life extends far beyond conventional novels or films. Story. . . . dominates human life" (p. 11). "Clever scientific studies involving beepers and diaries suggest that an average daydream is about fourteen seconds long and the we have about 2,000 of them per day. In other words, we spend about half of our waking hours—one-third of our lives on earth—spinning fantasy stories."

Welcome to the amazing science of story and of how to use it!

■ ■ ■

—— A STORY (ACTUALLY MY STORY) ——

We begin in a city park sandbox in Alameda, California, a suburb of San Francisco, tucked in along the shore of the bay next to Oakland. It was the early 1980s, and I led a small research team at Lawrence Berkeley Lab. But I sat in that sandbox because I was assigned to shepherd my almost five-year-old nephew-in-law-to-be through the afternoon.

I was 35. We had run and frolicked across the park and played every game you can play on the old steam train engine. It was time for him slow down. But "slow down" was not in his nature. Until that day, when I chanced to say, "Let's flop into the sandbox and I'll tell you a story."

And he sat, looking expectantly at me as if to say, "Let's go. Get started. Make it a good one." If you had asked me that day, I would have said that no, story was not in my makeup. I was a science guy. During almost three years of grad school I never touched the half of the Oregon State University library that housed stories and literature. I only knew the science stacks. Before that, I had graduated from West Point (undergraduate degree in general engineering). During four years of constant course work and 185 semester hours of classes, the only "art" class I took was The Art of Napoleonic Tactics. I then spent five years in the army testing and developing satellite communications systems. I was a confirmed science/engineering mind.

Back to the park. I started to make up a story. I didn't much care where it went or if it made sense. If he was willing to sit and listen, I was going to ramble on. My goal was child management, not storytelling.

But an interesting thing happened. As soon as I started the story, other children . . . just materialized and flopped down in the sand to listen. It was almost as if they had been hiding under the sand waiting for someone to start a story, at which time they popped out to listen.

As if they could sense the unique vibrations of a story in the air, children from across the park streamed over—as if it were unthinkable that they would willingly miss a story.

Soon the adults who had brought those children to the park began to drift over to see why their child was hunkered down in the sandbox with this man who wasn't at work in the middle of the day when he should have been. They'd smile in relief, "Ohhh, he's just telling stories." And then most of those adults stayed to listen.

They had missed much of the story. There was no guarantee that the story was going anywhere. They didn't care. They somehow perceived in a few seconds that it was a story, and they tuned in to listen.

It became a regular pattern of our trips to the park. I would often look up from these stories I was making up just to keep my nephew-in-law-to-be quiet for a few minutes and find rings of 80 to 100 people jammed around, listening.

Then came one specific day when it hit me. Midway through a story I had one of those rare life epiphanies. In a flash, it hit me. If I sat in that sandbox and *read* any of the reports that I was paid what I thought was pretty good money by the Department of Energy to create, *none* of these people would stay to listen.

They gathered and lingered because—even just strolling past—they perceived that it was a *story*. Instantly they treated it differently. Instantly they were engaged. They paid attention as they would *not* if it had not been perceived to be a story.

I realized that day that our brains automatically treat stories differently than we do any other kind or form of narrative information. We pay more attention to stories. We visualize them more vividly. We remember them more accurately and completely. We recall them more easily. Over the past few years, I have been able to see it on EEG scans. Different (and additional) sensory and experiential regions of the brain light up when test subjects perceive that they are listening to a story.

We are all hooked on stories because that is the way our brains are wired and our minds are programmed. Yet, most people take this most powerful of communications tools for granted. We tend to overlook—to dismiss—story's tremendous power and potential. It's like comedian Rodney Dangerfield might have said, "Stories just don't get no respect!"

We don't give stories enough credit for what they accomplish for us. Stories can permanently change attitudes and beliefs. Simple stories become the focal points that frame societal debates. They can blast like chain lightning through entire populations, leaving no one untouched and unchanged. Stories have won (and lost) national elections. Scan the history of the presidential bids of Michael Dukakis (1988) and John Kerry (2004) if you doubt that statement. It only took one effective attack story to sink each of those campaigns. Stories have started wars. They have ended wars. They have reshaped lives and futures.

I was still a rookie storyteller when I was invited back to an elementary school. It had been 13 months since my first appearance to perform a pair of storytelling assemblies. As I entered the school, a second grade girl passed me, heading for the front door. She stopped and said, "Oh, you're the man who told us stories last year." I was flattered that she remembered. But she then proceeded (as kids will) to tell me one of the stories I had told in that first assembly.

And she got it exactly right! It was a ten-minute story; and she got it all right: the characters, goals, struggles, conflicts, climax, resolution, and many of the details. It was one of my original stories. She had only heard it once in her life. Her only instructions at the time were to walk into the multipurpose room, sit down on the floor, and be quiet. Still, 13 months later, with no prompting, the entire story flooded back into her mind—accurately and vividly.

How many things do you remember—accurately—for a year? It happens regularly with stories.

I performed at the Mariposa (California) Storytelling Festival several years in a row back in the late 1980s. A decade later, I returned to Mariposa to conduct workshops at the high school. During a break, one of the senior girls asked me if I could help her find the name of a story she had once heard. She told me the story. It was one of mine—another original story. She didn't remember me. But she accurately remembered the story. I was able to look back in my files to see when I had told it. She had heard that story once, during an evening performance at the festival—as an eight-year-old girl—and still accurately and vividly remembered it a decade later!

If remembering something accurately for a year is surprising, what about remembering it for a *decade*? On just *one* hearing? The books on marketing I have read talk about how many times a customer must be exposed to a product message before she is likely to recall it when making a purchase decision. That number usually hovers around five to seven exposures. Effective stories are remembered and accurately recalled on *one* exposure. So is the information imbedded in those stories. That makes stories a most attractive and effective road to getting the communications results you need and want.

Having been gifted with that flash epiphany in the park, I quit my science career and declared to the world that I was now a storyteller! My greater family assumed that, me being 36 by this time, I was having a mid-life crisis. They all thought I had lost my mind. None of them could conceive that "telling stories" could be a career. Yet, recent research has shown that a surprisingly large percentage of the jobs in our country require—even hinge on—the ability to tell stories: to team members, to funders, to associates, to customers, to clients, to shift workers. Most work positions in this country depend on the ability to tell stories!

When I entered the community of American storytellers in 1982, I was the only working teller with an advanced degree in science. I was instantly pigeonholed as the one to gather the research to prove how powerful and important storytelling is.

That ongoing research effort led to invites to present workshops at a number of science agencies. One of these, at Goddard Space Flight Center in late 2006, changed my career. After a 90-minute talk for science writers on the use of stories in science reporting, a senior NASA manager challenged me to prove it. If I claimed that stories were a more effective way to communicate science results to the public, he dared me to back up my claim with some proof.

I was backed into a corner and had no choice except to force a smile and say, "Sure. No problem." At the time I thought, as did the entire storytelling community, that there existed no hard evidence to use and that I would have to rely on the great mass of available anecdotal evidence.

Two years of research and 150,000 pages later, I was blown away by the depth and breadth of available relevant, peer-reviewed, credible, quantitative research that supported the case I was tasked to produce. We thought there would be a desperate dearth of hard science. But in fact I found just the opposite. I found an avalanche of relevant research that spoke to how and why the human brain and mind relate to, process, and make sense out of incoming narrative and experience in specific story terms and elements. Collectively they showed exactly why people stopped in the park to listen and why I held their attention and focus—even with rambling, mediocre stories.

That research became my book *Story Proof*. Over the four years since the publication of that book, I have been gifted with opportunities to extend and refine that research with work focused specifically on the relationship between the elements of effective story and the wiring and programming of the human brain/mind.

This leads me to Narrative Networks, a DARPA (the science research arm of the Department of Defense) study aimed at better understanding the neuroscience explaining how stories exert influence. I was lucky enough to be the only storyteller and story writer involved in this research. Our Narrative Networks research gave me access to a 24-channel EEG lab with video cameras, cardio and skin galvanic monitors, and even saliva swabs to measure dopamine and oxytocin levels (your body's natural feel-good drugs). And it gave me access to a series of test audiences on whom I could experiment by telling each a slightly different version of a story.

This work allowed me to test and to quantify in a controlled and precise way the individual elements of story structure and their effect on an audience's mind and brain. It is the updated results of this work that serve as the basis for the information in this book.

■ ■ ■

YOUR REAL JOB

Have you ever paused to consider what *your real job* is when you write a paper or present a talk or lesson?

Let's start with another related question: Where does your story happen? That may seem like odd wording. Still, it is definitely worth considering. When you give a talk, teach a lesson, tell a story, or write a paper, where does the real action "happen"? Not in your head. It happened there long ago as you developed the information and ideas you now want to share. It doesn't happen in your mouth when you speak or on the page as you write.

Stories happen in the mind of the audience member. That's where all of the action takes place that you work so hard to create. That's where your impact will be felt. You don't succeed unless you succeed inside your audience's mind. Your communication goals are met when you persuade, convince, teach, or influence the individuals in that audience; when you change their beliefs, attitudes, values, knowledge, or behavior. That's why it's important for you to understand how your audience hears and what happens inside their brain/mind once they get a hold of your words.

A Telling Example	*In the fall of 2002, I was on the road in a small Northern California town and wanted a cup of coffee while I waited for the local breakfast place to open up. I went inside a fast-food joint. At the counter I ordered a cup of decaf. The obnoxiously perky girl at the register (she looked 15 but was more likely 18 or 19) asked, "Senior discount?" I replied, "What's it worth?" She gushed, "It's only a quarter with the discount. You save 40 cents!"* *I said, "That's a great deal. But I gotta tell you. I'm not a senior. I'm only 55." With a slight dismissive wave and a big, helpful smile she beamed, "Oh, that's okay. You look plenty old enough to me!" (Yes, those are all actual quotes. I ran out to my car and wrote the whole thing down.)*

Imagine the difference between the story that ran in my mind and the extremely helpful customer service story that she thought she had said. I am sure that it never occurred to her that her story, as it arrived in my mind, was, "You look like a *really* old and decrepit person to me!" Yet, it was my mental version of her story that counted, not the one in her mind, or even the story as it came out of her mouth. Stories happen in the brain/mind of the receiver.

Back to your job. Your job is not to say what you want to say. It is not even to get the words right when you say it or write it. Research shows that we humans don't really hear the exact words you say, anyway. We really hear the gist. We then re-form that gist into words inside our own brains, using our own vocabulary. Then we ascribe our self-created personalized version back to the source, thinking that our own version is actually word for word, what the speaker said.

Your job is not to get your message or your information out there. It's not to put it on paper clearly and forcefully.

Your real job *is* to have listeners (or readers) accurately understand, remember, recall, and apply your messages and information to affect their beliefs, attitudes, knowledge, and behavior.

That is an entirely different task from just getting your thoughts out of your mouth or onto paper. Your real job is what introduces an essential role for stories. Enter sticky stories—stories that stick with audiences, stories that sway the audience, that hold onto them and won't let go.

More specifically, your ***real job*** is to make it *easy* for your audiences to accurately understand, remember, and apply your material. This is where the elements and tools of effective story structure become essential assets.

But let's be clear on the role of sticky stories in this process. Stories engage listeners and readers. Neural researchers differ a bit in their definitions of what engagement is and what it looks like in the human brain. Through one of the research projects I have been part of over the past two years, we were able to establish that engagement has a mandatory emotional component. We have defined engagement and related terms as:

Engagement:	Emotionally laden attention
Attention:	Dedicated mental focus over time
Influence:	Changing another person's beliefs, attitudes, values, knowledge, or behavior

We were able to show that emotional involvement and engagement exactly tracked with each other in neural lab experiments. When the physiologic and kinesthetic markers of engagement (when someone looked like they were fully engaged in a story) and when the neural signatures linked to engagement indicated that they were engaged, the neural markers for emotional involvement were always also present. When one set of markers declined, so did the other. When one increased, so did the other. Emotions and engagement are inexorably linked.

You will not fully engage your audiences with information alone. No one ever stormed Washington over a pie chart. The information, of course, must be there. But using story elements activates an emotional involvement. They make it seem "personal." That emotional involvement is a necessary component of full engagement. Engagement creates focused mental attention. And that is what you are after when you speak or when you write.

Let me offer one quick example of the difference between the information (the facts) and the power of the story once that emotional involvement has been activated, once story structure immerses the listener in the story and makes it feel personal.

I was invited to present a story workshop at a local nonprofit organization. They opened with a business meeting during which one of the officers projected a slide of two smiling Mexican nuns flanked by men holding a club banner and standing in front of a new washer and dryer. The officer said that because of the donations of this club (combined with those of three other clubs), they had purchased a new commercial washer and dryer for this Mexican orphanage. Polite applause trickled across the room. The officer said they needed more money to buy a similar unit for a second orphanage. Response was "muted."

Following my story structure workshop, that officer approached me and said that he now realized that he had blown it. He had jumped straight to the conclusion and had skipped the story.

What's the story? It is an orphanage for over 180 abandoned children and babies with AIDS. Most soiled their clothes so often that they had to sit naked on their beds all day waiting for clean clothes to wear. All the nuns could afford were low-end residential washers that soon broke from the prodigious wash loads. Behind the orphanage stood a field of rusting, broken washers and dryers. Trickles of contaminated water oozed from the towering mounds of dirty clothes and bedding. The stench hit visitors like a solid wall. The nuns were constantly ill from working in the fetid squalor. Rats ran rampant and seemed to own the place.

The four club volunteers (including that officer) who went down to install the new commercial washer and dryer fought red tape, inadequate power lines, corroded water lines, and inadequate drain systems. They worked, sweated, dug, and argued with indifferent officials for three weeks to get to that smiling picture in front of the new machines.

At a breakfast meeting of a sister club, that officer told "the story." He received $4,000 in checks, cash, and pledges that morning. That's the power of story engagement.

Taylor (1996, p. 132) wrote, "A story does what facts and statistics never can: it inspires and motivates. Expert storytellers translate complex ideas into practical examples laced with strong emotional connections. The audience tunes in because they see themselves woven into the story."

During a personal phone interview (March 2013), futurist Rolf Jensen predicted, "Companies will thrive on the basis of their stories and myths."

In workshops, I use the following summary list of what effective stories provide.

- Context
- Relevance
- Engagement
- Understanding
- Empathy
- Meaning
- Memory and recall

Impressive list. If you could accomplish each of those each time you spoke, you would quickly become a sought-after speaker. The acclaim would be equally laudatory if you could accomplish them each time you wrote. More importantly, notice that each of these highly desirable achievements happens inside the mind of the receiver of your story.

This brings me to a final aspect of your real job. You can't identify what makes effective stories so effective by looking at the *stories*. You must look at the human **brain** and see how it processes and remembers effective stories differently from other narratives. After one more part of this book that sets stories within their proper context, we will turn to several parts on exactly what does happen in each listener's brain and mind.

■ ■ ■

PAY ATTENTION! STORY IS AN ECONOMIC EVENT

Think of your storytelling—your talks, lecture, articles, and other writing—as actual economic events, as buying and selling, as an exchange of valuable goods. You are the seller. Your audience members are the hopeful buyers. Picture yourself as the owner of a stall there in the bustling Information Mall trying to entice information shoppers as they drift past.

You are the seller of your teaching/influencing information and messages. In order to make that sale, you need to buy your target audience's attention. (We already know that if you don't hold their attention, you have wasted both your time and theirs. No influence, teaching, persuading, or inspiration is going to happen.)

You stand by the cash register of your Information Mall booth calling out like a classic midway barker, "Hurry, hurry, hurry! Step right up. Get your new and improved information. Guaranteed to change your life. Available right here; right now! Hurry, hurry, hurry!"

The eternal central sellers question is: *Is what I'm selling what my audience wants to buy?*

Do people arrive at your article, talk, lesson, or presentation already intent on buying your information, ideas, and message points? The research says no. There are well-established exceptions. However, in most cases people arrive not at all committed to buying what you want to sell. They arrive with arms skeptically folded over their chests and a "Go ahead, convince me" skeptical glare in their eyes.

So, what *do* they come ready to buy?

Pennebaker (2011, p. 104) said, "When people (characters) behave emotionally, it always demands our close attention." Emotion and attention are directly linked.

From Rose (2011, p. 8): "We know this much: people want to be immersed. They want to get involved in a story (to be engaged), to carve out a role for themselves (vicariously experience the story), to make it their own (to internalize and visualize the story)."

People are always ready to pay to be **engaged**, to be emotionally and personally immersed in your material. What currency do they use to pay for this engagement? They pay with their attention—the exact thing you want to buy.

Lisa Cron (2012, p. 4) described a recent brain imaging study reported in *Psychological Science* that revealed that the regions of the brain that process the sights, sounds, tastes, and movement of real life are activated when we're engrossed (engaged) in a compelling story. Stories fully engage audiences in the same way that real—life experiences do—something other narrative forms typically do not. It is that "just like I was really there" neural experience that people come to stories willing to buy and pay for with their attention.

Attention is the currency of this transaction. You want to pedal your information and you want to exert influence with it. They want to buy engagement. In order for them to plop their attention coins into your palm, they need the promise of engagement. Your ability to influence hitches along as a secondary bonus product thrown in (like Ginsu knives) when someone makes an engagement purchase and, thereby, *pays* attention to your material.

And this is where stories and story elements serve your purpose. Stories offer engagement to your hungry customers, who then shower you with attention in order to capture that experience of engagement. And voila! You have the opportunity to influence, which was your original goal.

A summary: Influence, your real job (remember that "influence" is the academic research term for teach, convince, or inspire), requires you to gather and hold attention. Buying attention requires you to offer engagement, which requires you to immerse your audience on an emotional level. You will intentionally adjust and manipulate the story elements of your material in order to control that emotional involvement and engagement. Story structures consistently evoke that emotional involvement, deeply and fully engage, and garner attention—thus allowing you to do your job.

■ ■ ■

PART II

STORY STATE OF MIND

THE MIND IS WHAT THE BRAIN DOES

Why dive into the gooey morass of brain/mind science? Why detour away from your story for a quick tour of the human brain—in particular, of the brain of the people (clients, students, employees, donors, etc.) who will hear your stories and whom you intend to influence? Simple. What their brain does with your story is critical to your success. Everything you want to accomplish with your stories happens in the receiver's brain. Your success or failure will be determined by what happens inside the three pounds of wiggly gray goo stuffed beneath the skull of your individual audience members.

The human brain has until quite recently been treated by researchers as a classic "black box" (the science term for a place we can't pry open to actually see what happens). We control what goes into the box and watch what comes back out to gain clues as to what happened inside the black box. We tell stories and then watch the listener's response. Then we scratch our heads and try to guess at what they did in their mind with the story text (how they processed it, how they made sense out of it, how they understood it, etc.) That investigative process is at the heart of the field of narratology (the academic study of narrative).

Being forced to study what the brain does without being able to actually watch it do what it does always reminds me of trying to analyze a family's Thanksgiving dinner by standing outside in the cold and peering in through the dining room window. From out there in the snow, you can list the dishes, count the people and their positioning around the table. You can record how many forks, knives, and wine glasses are set out. You can record the groceries that go in the day before and weigh the garbage carried out the day after. But you'll never really capture the smells, the energy, the taste, or the feeling of the meal as long as you are stuck outside treating the actual event as if it were locked in another black box.

Yet even the black box type of crude assessment of brain function is relatively new. Ancient Egyptian mummifiers saved what they thought were the important organs (liver, lungs, stomach, and intestines) in canopic jars that were carefully buried with the mummified body. The brain they pulled out through the nose with something like a crochet hook and threw it away as worthless.

As late as the mid-1700s, scientists believed that thought, intelligence, and consciousness happened almost anywhere in the human body other than in the brain. Some thought it happened in the heart. Others favored the intestines. Some chose the stomach. Others tried to prove that intelligence rested in the lungs. Those beliefs are the origins of phrases such as "Trust your gut." "What's your gut reaction?" and "Listen to your heart." When first used, those phrases meant "Stop and think about it!" It is amazing that so recently, the medical and scientific communities gave virtually no credit to the brain.

Not any more. Modern research technology has allowed us to sneak past the skull and watch human brains in action. Now we can literally watch your mental neurons collectively think! It is well worth your while to take a few minutes for a fast tour of the brain and how it performs its story magic with the story fodder you provide.

Much of this chapter is based on work by a handful of giants in the fields of developmental psychology, evolutionary biology, neural biology, and cognitive sciences: Pinker, Bransford, Bruner, Schank, Turner, Egan, Applebee, Anderson, Kotulak, Crossley, Lakoff and Johnson, and Fisher. I refer you to their excellent work for more general treatises on mental functioning. I have had to cull through the broader research by these scientists to locate the limited gems that pertain to the intersection of mind and story.

It is virtually impossible for us to be aware of our own story minds in action. Story thinking is how you *always* think and have *always* thought. Your brain is not wired to use nonstory thinking. In this way, story is like gravity. You know gravity is here. You know it pushes you down onto the earth. But you aren't physically, consciously aware of that force or that push as you are of the weather. You can't feel gravity. Why? Because you have never known "*not* gravity" (weightlessness). Fish can't describe water because they have never experienced "*not* water."

However, we can set up artificial game situations to let you see your story mind in action. First, two quick demonstrations of how amazingly capable your gray goo is at juggling as many story balls as anyone can throw at it.

First, consider these two lines:

> *Person #1: Hello, Ken.*
> *Ken: Shhh! No, it's not me! I'm not here! It must be somebody else.*

You read this and begin to run possible mental scenarios to make both lines make sense—to create meaning. You assume that, 1) both lines *do* make sense and 2) are rational and relevant. To create meaning, you must invent (infer) goal and motive (and possible obstacles) for both characters. You must choose to completely disregard what Ken *literally* says and change its meaning 180 degrees in order to find a rational interpretation that will make it make sense. You create *stories* in order to create meaning and understanding.

That is an amazing amount of creative juggling for your brain to do—most of it in one small fraction of a second. Yet, you do that same trick so regularly it hardly merits any recognition.

Now picture eight of your friends. Picture them standing side-by-side singing "Happy Birthday." Picture them doing so while riding on elephants with clown-faced helium balloons tied to their tusks by golden thread . . . while the elephants dance across the deck of a yellow submarine . . . that is flying through the sky . . . past glowing purple clouds . . . that moo when they rain milk down upon the deck . . . while the uniformed captain stands atop the sub's conning tower carrying a spinning orange umbrella and salutes.

How did you mentally create those images? For most people that is trivially easy to do. Yet, it is a wondrous feat. You instantly created images that never existed. You can't possibly have seen or experienced most of what you just created. Those images didn't come from your memory banks. Yet, the creating was likely as easy (or even easier) than accurately recalling the face, clothes, and body posture of those eight friends. The mental mechanisms you use to create story-based images are truly remarkable.

And they are dizzyingly active. They pounce on every opportunity to envision, interpret, embellish, adjust, alter, and augment incoming information from sensory organs. Every person who listens to you or who reads what you write does it, too. With every sentence and every bit of information you provide.

■ ■ ■

THE GOO THAT LETS YOU THINK

Ball your hands into fists and hold them together, knuckles touching with thumbs on top and pinkie fingers on the bottom. That's about how big your brain is. No wires, sparks, batteries, or flashes. Just a wrinkly, soft to the touch lump that is 85 percent water and typically weighs less than three pounds. But that wobbly glob controls everything you do, everything you feel, everything you think, everything you dream and wish. Your brain faithfully performs thousands of functions every second that you are alive.

That typical brain contains 100 billion brain cells (100,000,000,000)—about the same as the number of stars in the Milky Way. That's also a million times more brain cells than a fruit fly has and has 10 times as many as most monkeys. Each cell is linked by synapses to as many as 100,000 others. That means your brain has created over 500 trillion (500,000,000,000,000) wiggling string-like fibers called axons and dendrites that connect with other neurons at junctions called synapses. These synapses are awash with neurotransmitters and hormones that modulate the transmission of electro-chemical signals. Synapses constantly form and dissolve, weakening and strengthening in response to new experiences.

A typical brain neuron receives input from thousands of other cells, some of which inhibit rather than encourage the neuron's firing. The neuron may, in turn, encourage or discourage firing by some of those same cells in complex positive and negative feedback loops. Somehow, through this freeway maze of links, loops, and electric traffic jams, we each manage to think, to perceive, to consider, to imagine, to remember, to react, and to respond.

If you'd like to read more about brain structure I recommend Pinker (2000), Kotulak (1999), Newquist (2004), Horgan (2004), or Kruglinski (2005).

■ ■ ■

Paul Broca (in 1861) was the first to prove that different parts of the brain have specific mental functions. Working with a man named "Tan," Broca identified a small area of the brain (Broca's area) that controls speech. In 1874 Carl Wernicke identified an area just behind Broca's that helps people understand language. Wernicke's area seems to have a role in looking up words and funneling them to other areas (notably Broca's) that assemble words into blocks to construct meaning.

The key take-away from this is that language processing (either audible or from written words) is not part of the conscious mind. It all happens in the lower back portion of the brain in the subconscious mind.

Pinker (2000) was saying the same thing when he stated, "A very gross anatomy of the language sub-organs within the perisylvian [*subconscious lower back portion of the brain*] might be: front of the persylvian (including Broca's area): grammatical processing; rear of the perisylvian (including Wernicke's and the three-lobe junction): the sound of words, especially nouns, and some aspects of their meaning."

Further, it is important to note that the frontal lobes, which house the circuitry for decision making and conscious thought, are not directly connected to your sensory organs—or even to the brain areas that process raw sensory input. Instead, most of what reaches your conscious mind is what neuroscientists call **highly processed** input coming from regions one or more stops downstream from the first sensory areas (Crick and Koch 1995). It is these areas of the subconscious mind that first process and massage incoming information from sensory organs (ears and eyes) and turn it into something that makes sense. These subconscious brain regions are the key to understanding what makes effective stories powerful, moving, and influential.

Unconscious portions of our human brains process raw sensory input and pass it to intermediate processing areas of the brain. These areas (also in the unconscious portions of our brains) are the exact areas that are activated when humans create stories (Pinker 2000; Newquist 2004; Kotulak 1999). The output of these regions is fed to the conscious mind for consideration. In other words, the brain converts raw experience into story form and then considers, ponders, remembers, and acts on the self-created story, not the actual input experience!

Edleman and Tononi (2000) concluded, "These unconscious aspects of mental activity play a fundamental role in shaping and directing our conscious experience."

Now we arrive at the bottom line of this brain anatomy, at the point where it begins to explain our predilection to story. The brain adapts over time to best meet human needs.

Consider how long, in Western civilizations, have people *en masse* been able to read? The answer is only a couple hundred years. Less than half of the American colonists were literate when they decided to revolt against King George.

You might ask, "So what?" The "so what" is that reading is a very new human activity when measured on an evolutionary scale. Reading is so new that there is no area or center in the brain devoted to reading. That's why reading must be taught. As it is learned, reading steals space from a number of regions scattered across the brain. Notice, for example, that children learn to speak on their own quite quickly and quite well. The brain contains centers devoted to speech. But there is no neural reading center.

What about writing? Generally, Sumerian is recognized as the oldest written language and dates to around 5000 BCE (7,000 years ago). True, symbols that look like writing have been found at the Jiahu site in China carved into tortoise shells that date from around 8,500 years ago. But there aren't enough of these symbols to establish the existence of a written language. Writing, again, is a very new human undertaking, one that has not yet set up a permanent home site in the brain.

What about storytelling? Even the most conservative evolutionary biologists I could find agree that humans had the complex language and social organization necessary to indicate that they shared stories at least 100,000 years ago. I believe that new skull findings from Africa will soon push that number to at least 300,000 years ago.

Our early humanoid ancestors told stories. They shared stories. They built important historical, factual, societal (tribal), and ecological information into the stories they told. They remembered that information in story form—in human memory. (Remember, there was no writing, no other way to archive and retrieve those essential stories.)

■ ■ ■

LET ME INTRODUCE ... YOUR NEURAL STORY NET (NSN)

Evolutionary biologists first proposed this idea. It has since been extensively tested by developmental psychologists, biologists, and other neural scientists. 100,000 years of story dominance in how humans interact, communicate, and archive and recall essential information has *evolutionarily rewired human brains* so that we are all born hardwired to think, to understand, to make sense in and through specific story terms and story concepts. For more on this important concept, see Nelson (2003), Donald (1991), Plotkin (1982), Tomasello (1995), Bruner (2003), or Pinker (2000).

Why are stories so powerful and alluring and engaging? Because that's the way your brain is wired! We are preprogrammed from before birth to seek specific story information when we try to understand and create meaning from the world around us. We think in story form. We make sense in story form. We create meaning in story form. We remember and recall in stories. This drive to focus on story information can be seen in babies only a few months old.

When I say that we are hardwired to think in story terms, I am speaking literally, not metaphorically. Those neural connections physically exist and link together the neural subregions that form a fixed network of brain regions that fire together to process incoming signals. I have started calling this network the *Neural Story Net*—the regions you use to create the specific elements of your stories. I spent a chapter in my book *Story Proof* describing the development and dominance of this neural circuit. Rather than repeat that information here, I refer you to that book if you'd like to read more on this development.

These story-generating subregions of the brain are hardwired together so that they fire together to deal with incoming information. You can see the relevant areas light up on EEG scans. You can see the same areas light up when people are prompted to create stories—one story element at a time. This Neural Story Net is the specific part of the brain that undertakes that initial processing of incoming signals and that then sends "highly processed" information—in story form—to the conscious mind.

Story *IS* how we learn and how we are motivated, inspired, and persuaded. As Gottschall (2012, p. xiv) says, "Humans: the great ape with the storytelling mind." We are truly *Homo narratus,* story animals.

The important questions for those who want to effectively use stories in their communications are: What does the Neural Story Net do, and how does it do it?

■ ■ ■

Here are two key research findings that, I think, lie at the heart of the central importance of the Neural Story Net.

1. Where the NSN sits. Let's say you read something. That information travels as an electrical signal down the optic nerve to the lower back part of the brain. There the signal scatters to almost 30 separate tiny subareas that interpret the electrical impulses as squiggly lines, then as letters and words, and then as a visual thing that acquires dimension. (Oh, it's a chair, or an apple, or a human . . .) Other areas try to identify more specific information about it and then send their findings to the *fusiform gyrus*, a small area responsible for basic visual recognition identification (a spider, my wife, a folding chair, my boss . . .).

Now this signal goes in two interlinked directions. First it travels to the *amygdala* (the gateway to the limbic system) to add emotional response. (Uh-oh. I hate my boss!) It also lights up the rest of the Neural Story Net that tries to make sense out of this image of your boss appearing at this time in this sequence of visual images.

Note that this visual image has not yet traveled to your conscious mind in the frontal cortex. It is still rumbling about in the subconscious regions of your brain. The same pattern occurs with audio signals.

2. The NSN is that part of the brain that holds the task of initially making sense out of this stream of incoming visual and audio information.

Developmental psychologists have carefully and exhaustively described and documented this supreme drive to make sense of incoming information. Over the past several years, I have started calling it the *Make Sense Mandate*. Recent research (including my own as part of the Narrative Networks project) has confirmed that this Make Sense Mandate is an incredibly strong and dominant force in human mental activity. If you can't make sense out of it, you tend to ignore it. At some evolutionary time in the past—and this is the key point—the job of making sense out of incoming narrative and experiential information was assigned to the Neural Story Net. Yes, that hard-wired group of story-generating subregions in your brain—all located deep in the subconscious part of your brain—is required to make sense out of incoming information.

How does the NSN do it? It uses story structures.

Here is the final kicker (one that I will demonstrate in a moment). If incoming information does not—on its own—make sense to your NSN, those subregions of your mind that make up this network rush in to make it make sense.

To do that, your NSN is routinely willing to:

- Change (*even reverse*) factual information
- Make assumptions

- Create new information
- Ignore parts of the provided information
- Infer connections and information
- Infer motive, intent, and significance
- Invent new information and detail

Your friendly NSN will do whatever it needs to do to make the incoming information make sense! If it can't make sense out of it, your conscious mind is cued to ignore it.

Put those extraordinary findings together and what do you get?

1. The NSN lies *between* your sensory organs (eyes and ears) and your conscious mind. Nothing reaches your conscious mind (and your memory) without first being massaged into story shape by your NSN.
2. You turn all incoming narrative and experiential information into story form *before* it reaches your conscious mind.
3. What reaches your conscious mind is always your own story-based interpretation of what your sensory organs actually recorded.
4. When you talk, the story they hear and see in their conscious minds *is not* the story you said! Their conscious minds hear the story their NSN created *based* on the story you actually provided.

We are truly story animals: *Homo narratus*. Your story-creating mental apparatus lies between your conscious mind and the outside world. We think in story terms because we are hardwired and preprogrammed to do so. We invent—as needed—story material to make the world around us make sense because that is the way our brains are wired to make sense.

This revelation explains a conundrum that—for some odd reason—has always bugged me. Picture this scene. A busy intersection; two cars slam into each other. Fire and severe injuries. Ambulances rush in and cart away the dead and injured. Then police interview the witnesses to find out what happened. They find eight eyewitnesses . . . and get eight different stories! It always seemed so baffling to me. Why would seven of them get it wrong? Was the point that seven out of eight witnesses aren't very observant? Is it that seven out of eight of us lie to the police?

No! The answer is that all eight of those witnesses—at an automatic, subconscious level—changed what their sensory organs recorded into story form in order to make it make sense *to them* before their NSN passed the information to the conscious mind. The story that finally reached their conscious minds is the information that they then dutifully reported to the police.

Each one of those eight witnesses, with their radically different stories, could pass lie detector tests. Those tests measure what exists in the conscious brain. The work of story conversion happened long before the conscious mind took hold of this information.

That is the power and influence of this Neural Story Net. It defines and creates your reality!

Think of your Neural Story Net as a prism ... you know, those triangular prisms that diffract light, separating it into the component color bands of a rainbow. The light that emerges from a prism is not the same as the light that went in.

Same with your NSN. The story that emerges from your NSN (racing to your conscious mind) is not the same story that entered from your sensory organs. Just as a prism distorts light, the NSN distorts incoming information in order to make it make sense.

More than that, think of the NSN as blinders. Why? As we shall see in the next section, the NSN sucks information from your Banks of Prior Knowledge (your total past learning and experience) in order to make things make sense. Your NSN grabs the most likely scenario—according to your past experience—in that process. In so doing, it ignores all possibilities that do not conform to that "most likely explanation" based on your personal Banks of Prior Knowledge. The bulging raft of other possible explanations never occurs to you. You are shielded from considering them by your NSN's need to jump instantly to the "this-is-what-makes-the-most-sense-to-me" version.

Here is what research over the past decade has shown.

> **When you use "effective" story structure, you minimize the distortion created by the NSN of your intended audience.**

The story (and the associated information) that arrives at the conscious mind of your audience is both much closer to, and more accurately reflective of, the version you actually delivered.

That is an amazingly important statement for me to be able to make, and the science is there to back it up. If you craft your stories based on the elements of effective story structure, your messages, your themes, and your information will arrive more accurately into the conscious minds and memories of your intended audience.

A quick review ... because *this is really the heart of this book*. In order to persuade, influence, inspire, or teach you must:

1. Engage your target audience.
2. Hold their attention.
3. Get through their NSN without serious distortion or alteration to your information and message.

Effective story structure lies at the heart of all three of these tasks.

A quick analogy from the world of optic lasers. Engineers who send site-to-site laser beams find that the miles of atmosphere between the transmission and receiver dishes distorts the information carried on that beam. Particulate, humidity, and pollutants all degrade the signal quality so that the information received is not quite the same as the information transmitted. Big problem. To fix it, engineers place the corrective lenses and filters in front of the beam at the source to compensate for, to correct for, the atmosphere's distortive havoc.

Effective story structure is your set of corrective filters to compensate for the distortions the audience's Neural Story Net (NSN) would otherwise create and better ensures that the version of your information and messaging that reaches their conscious minds is as clear, sharp, and accurate as you intended.

And now it's time to demonstrate your story mind in action to see what I mean.

Consider these two spoken lines:

> *Person #1: Where's John?*
> *Person #2: Well . . . I didn't want to say anything. **But** . . . I saw a green VW parked in front of Carol's.*

If there is someone with you, explain two things to that person. (If you are alone, say your explanation out loud.)

1. What's going on here?
2. What is the relationship between the four people mentioned (Person #1 and person #2, who both speak; someone named John; and someone named Carol)?

Were you able to make these lines make sense? What did your mind have to do in order to answer my two questions?

Three concepts about your NSN's mode of operation ring out here:

1. Did you say, "No, I can't possibly answer your two questions; you didn't give me sufficient information"? In truth, I didn't. All of your answers to my questions were your inventions. More specifically, they were the inventions of your NSN in its efforts to meet its Make Sense Mandate. The relationships you think are obvious are all your own invention. They are "obvious" to you not because they are correct but because they make the given text make sense to you.

2. Notice how willing you were to disregard (or radically alter) the *literal* information you were given if doing so helped you make it make sense. Person #2 was asked about a person (John) and talked about a car. Clearly—if you accept at face value the *literal* information you were given (and the point I am making is that we never do)—you would have to conclude that person #2 either didn't hear or has lost all touch with reality.

   But you didn't conclude that. That doesn't make good sense to you. So you instantly changed the meaning of person #2's comment by improvising something that didn't exist in the original text. (John drives a green VW.)

Notice also that as soon as you read person #2's opening statement ("Well . . . I didn't want to say anything"), you exactly reversed its meaning. You instantly assumed that person #2 couldn't wait to blurt out this bit of juicy gossip. Again, this is your NSN at work, struggling to make incoming information make sense to you.

3. Your NSN acts just like blinders. In its rush to make new information make sense, your NSN forces you to ignore a wide host of possible explanations. For example, you assumed that person #1 and person #2 are in the same space and are talking to each other. It doesn't say that. These could just be two sequential taps on an NSA galactic surveillance log. These people could be 4,000 miles apart. But that doesn't make sense to you because you have been trained to assume that information presented sequentially on the page must fit together. That makes sense. So you ignore all other possibilities.

Think of all the possible interpretations of person #2's lines that you ignored as you rushed to make it make sense. There could easily be dozens, and any one of those could easily be the intended meaning.

Remember: people do this same mental gymnastics routine every time they are exposed to your information, to your messages. The writing rule of thumb is: If it is possible for your audience to misinterpret what you write, they will!

Consider this next set of lines.

> *Person #1: Hi **John**.*
>
> *Person #2: Shhhh! I'm not here! You never saw me. I'm not here!*
>
> *Person #1: It's okay. **Carol**'s gone home.*

Instantly, you can make perfect sense out of this scene. Right? You assume that person #2 is John. You assume that what John is really saying is that he doesn't want to run into Carol and doesn't want her to know that he is here (wherever they are). You assume that person #1 is a good friend and understands this and also knows that Carol has left (wherever they are) and has gone home. So now John is safe.

You likely were able to invent that interpretation as quickly as you read the three lines. You were instantly willing to say, "I know what these lines *really* mean." Yet, that is not at all what the lines actually say. In order to make it make sense to you, you radically changed what the author literally wrote.

Do people do that to you when you write? When you speak? The answer is, "Yes!" unless you guide them to make sense *your* way by using the elements of effective story structure.

Consider: Nothing in the text I provided says that person #2 is John. Nothing says that person #2 is thinking about (or worried about) Carol. If you take person #2's lines literally—and, again, my point is that we tend ***not*** to do that—you could only conclude that this poor person has severe mental problems and has lost all touch with reality. Clearly person #2 is *here*. And clearly person #1 *has* seen person #2— is even looking at him right now, for goodness sake! But that's not what your NSN fed to your conscious mind. Why? It doesn't make good sense.

One final demonstration. Consider these three statements:

> *He went to the store.*
>
> *Fred died.*
>
> *Sharon went hungry and wept*

Can't you feel yourself wanting to connect these three statements into a make-sense story? It's almost an overpowering urge to fit them together into a single narrative that makes sense. Notice that, for example, once you have read all three sentences, you automatically assume that "He" in the first sentence is Fred. It makes sense. However, in so doing, you were quite willing to violate the laws of English. Those laws specifically state that a pronoun ("he") can refer only to a noun that precedes it. You don't care. The laws of English don't stand a chance when they come up against the Make Sense Mandate!

Conclusion: The Make Sense Mandate is an incredibly powerful force in the minds of every person with whom you want to communicate. It is driven by the Neural Story Net's story-based structure, and it dominates the way every living person interacts with, and interprets, the world around them.

Before we examine the specific story-based informational elements that the NSN requires (and uses) in order to fulfill its Make Sense Mandate, we must address a lingering question . . . ***How do we do it?*** How does the NSN perform these mental gymnastics? Where does the NSN turn in order to invent the information it thinks is missing in a block of incoming information?

■ ■ ■

BANK ON IT: YOUR BANKS OF PRIOR KNOWLEDGE

It's important to understand just how a person's Neural Story Net (NSN) goes about its storied business. How and from where does the NSN find and create all that it so inventively creates?

Let's start with a demonstration. Consider these two sentences:

John felt lonely.
He rang the neighbor's doorbell.

Notice how comfortable you are fitting those two sentences together? That points out two central principles of the NSN:

1. You assume that all provided narrative information *does* make sense and *does* belong together.
2. You are willing to—actually, you expect to—be given only partial information.

The result? Your NSN is willing to—and *expects* to—infer, assume, elaborate, interpret, project, and jump to conclusions. It is likely a holdover survival tactic from the old fight-or-flight early days of humanoids.

Just look at what you did with John and his neighbor's doorbell:

1. We assume, and try to forcibly construct, a logical linkage between the two sentences.
2. We assume that John doesn't like feeling lonely. (a problem)
3. We assume that he wanted company. (a goal)
4. We assume that John likes the neighbor enough to want to be with him or her. (a character personality trait)
5. We assume that he believes that company will relieve his loneliness. (a motive for the goal)
6. We assume that he went next door and rang the bell in order to achieve that goal. (struggles—actions—to achieve goal resolution)

We assume; we assume; we assume!

The two given sentences say nothing about any of that information. Yet, they are logical, reasonable assumptions. If you continued to envision this growing story, you'd typically begin to infer the nature of the relationship between John and his neighbor. You'd begin to picture John's mood and the facial and body expressions that would probably go with it.

Reasonable as those assumptions and inferences might be, they are just that: the listener's own invention—not truth or fact. It could just as easily be true that feeling lonely makes John feel mean. He could have gone next door to lean on the doorbell hoping to torment the poor, elderly, bedridden man who had just come home from the hospital after breaking a hip in a fall.

Why didn't that scenario pop into your mind? Why did you jump first to an explanation that better fit our social norm? It's because that norm most likely matches the vast majority of your experiences.

■ ■ ■

── PUTTING YOUR BANKS TO WORK ──

What you invent, infer, assume, and project comes from your cumulative experiences: from you **Banks of Prior Knowledge**.

By definition, your Banks of Prior Knowledge are your sum total banks of existing knowledge and experience about a relevant topic. They are the sum total of everything you have learned and experienced, what you know and believe. You dredge information from your Banks of Prior Knowledge in order to fill in gaps in the incoming information and patch together a coherent and meaningful story.

New information arrives from your eyes or ears, and your mind calls down to your memory vaults for someone to check the files on this particular topic. That runner opens the right file drawer and thumbs through the manila folders until he reaches the one corresponding to the informational topic at hand.

The runner races back out of your memory vault and hands the folder over to your processing center. If that folder is empty, you say, "I don't know anything about this topic" and tend to use that as an excuse to ignore the incoming information. If the folder contains information, you use that existing information to create **context** for the new stuff. (*CONTEXT*: "The surrounding parts that determine meaning; background.") Context defines how this new information relates to what you already know and believe.

You use these same Banks of Prior Knowledge to decide if this new information is **relevant**. That is, if it is significant to you, if it likely means something to you, if it is *important* to you. (*RELEVANCE*: "Implying close relationship or importance.") Research studies suggest that if you lack context and relevance for incoming information, you are unlikely to pay attention to it. Other studies show that context and relevance are critical to accurate memory and recall.

What if the topic is new, unfamiliar, to your intended audience? What if they do not possess relevant file folders of information on some topic in their prior knowledge warehouse? This is certainly a common situation in classroom settings. Effective story structure *itself* creates sufficient context and relevance to make initial information in a new topic stick.

It's much like the marines during World War II landing on enemy-held Pacific islands to create an initial beachhead. Once the beachhead existed, other troops and supplies could flow in. Stories are much like those marines. The allure and relevance of story itself creates an initial mental beachhead for the first bits of topical information. Once those are lodged in active memory banks, they become the prior knowledge that creates the context and relevance to allow additional topical information to flow!

You use your Banks of Prior Knowledge every minute of every day to interpret what happens around you. Let's look at your Prior Knowledge in action.

I am going to show you seven groups of letters. The groups are small. They total only 20 letters. I want you to time yourself and see if you can memorize all seven groups of letters in 10 seconds.

If you think you can, have someone else time you. When you are ready, turn the page and start. After 10 seconds, turn the page again.

J   FKFB   INAT   OUP   SNA   SAI   RS

How'd you do? Did you learn all seven groups? The average I find is around four of the seven.

Why was it hard? You know all of the letters, so no real learning was involved.

It was hard because you have no context for these random groups of letters. They are not relevant to you. Thus, remembering and recalling is a struggle.

All I have to do is change the spaces between letters so that the new groupings match existing files in your Banks of Prior Knowledge. That existing knowledge and experience creates context and relevance for these revised letter groups, and you could easily remember them for days.

Again, all I will change is the spacing between letter groups—not the letters themselves or their order.

Ready? Go ahead and turn the page.

JFK   FBI   NATO   UPS   NASA   IRS

It's the same letters.

(J FKFB INAT OUP SNA SAI RS)

What's different? The new spacing creates letter groups for which you have prior knowledge and thus, context and relevance. Now memory is laughably easy. That's the power of context and relevance.

Here is another demo. Look at these seven sentences just long enough to read them. Then turn the page.

John walked on the roof.

Bill picked up the eggs.

Pete hid the ax.

Jim flew the kite.

Frank built the boat.

Harvey flipped the electric switch.

Ted wrote the play.

Do you remember all seven sentences? You shouldn't have had any trouble with comprehension. They are all simple declarative sentences.

Do you remember who built the boat? Who flew the kite? Why is memory and recall so difficult? No context and relevance. All I have to do is change the *name* used in each sentence in order to tap into your Banks of Prior Knowledge and create context and relevance—and memory becomes laughable easy.

> *Santa Claus walked on the roof.*
>
> *The Easter Bunny picked up the eggs.*
>
> *George Washington hid the ax.*
>
> *Benjamin Franklin flew the kite.*
>
> *Noah built the boat.*
>
> *Thomas Edison flipped the electric switch.*
>
> *William Shakespeare wrote the play.*

That's what context and relevance do for you. They make incoming information meaningful. It is always worth making sure you help your audience establish context and relevance for your information.

One last demonstration to show how prior knowledge and story structure merge in your mind. Consider this paragraph:

> *A thirsty ant went to the river. He was carried away by the rush of the stream and was about to drown. A dove, sitting in a tree overhanging the water, plucked a leaf. The leaf fell into the stream close to the ant, and the ant climbed onto it. The ant floated safely to the bank. Shortly afterward, a bird catcher came and laid a trap in the tree. The ant bit and stung him on the foot. In pain, the bird catcher threw down his trap. The noise made the dove fly away.*

Here's what typically happens when you read a paragraph like this. First you call up prior knowledge on physics, ecology, and biology. You know, for example, that ants walk, that they do need water, that they can float on the surface for a while (surface tension), but that eventually they will sink and drown since they can't survive underwater fish-style. Good so far. You have context for this story, and the story information is consistent with how your Banks of Prior Knowledge describe the world of ants.

And the same is true for the dove. As soon as your Banks of Prior Knowledge have cleared this paragraph and have said that it is consistent with your existing beliefs and world view, your Neural Story Net kicks in with story structure in order to make it relevant, meaningful, and worth your time and attention.

You assume things like, "The dove plucked the leaf *on purpose*." You assume a goal for the dove. Story structure now dictates to you that the ant owes a favor to the dove that must be repaid. So, in order to make the paragraph make sense, you assume that the bird catcher set a trap for the dove (the paragraph doesn't say that) and that the ant bit him on the foot **on purpose** in order to repay its obligation to the dove.

The dove flies away. Both are saved. Karmic balance has been restored. It has meaning, and all is well.

That's the way your NSN shuffles story structure and prior knowledge together in its attempt to create relevance and meaning.

For contrast, compare what your mind did with the ant paragraph to how it treats this one.

> *Pete argued that data gathered from a NASA voyage to Venus called into question current theories about the formation of our solar system. Part of his talk emphasized the importance of mass spectrometers. He then discussed the isotopes of argon 36 and argon 38 and noted that they were of higher density than expected. He also cited the high values of neon found in the atmosphere. He has a paper that is already written, but he is aware of the need for further investigation as well.*

Whereas you readily envisioned and "understood" the ant-dove paragraph (even though that understanding came from your own story-based creations), you probably didn't envision or try to fully understand the paragraph about astronomer Pete. Why? No context. You are extremely unlikely to have any prior experience with flights to Venus or with either of the isotopes mentioned. No context; no relevance. So you never fired up your story mind to create meaning. You had already decided that this paragraph doesn't have meaning for you and decided not to pay with your attention to envision and understand it.

If *you* don't anticipate, and build from, each audience's Banks of Prior Knowledge, a significant portion will treat your material in the same way you treated the paragraph about Pete. Effective story crafting begins with audience modeling.

■ ■ ■

FAMILY STORIES

Have you ever shared a holiday with another family and noticed that their family stories are always more boring than yours? They, of course, think the same thing about your family stories. Why is that?

It is because whenever you tell (or write) a story, you intentionally omit all information you know that your audience already holds in common.

It only makes sense. If I am going to tell a story about an ant (or a squirrel, or a balloon), I don't have to pause for a detailed anatomical and functional description of the thing I want to talk about. I name it, trust that your Banks of Prior Knowledge already hold sufficient information on that thing to create context and relevance, and get on with my story.

For family stories, the information the family already holds in common is, of course, character information. Everyone in the family already knows the characters. When I was growing up, anyone who announced that they had an Uncle Ev story drew a big and eager crowd. He was the family wild one, a magnet for the most amazing events and happenings. The teller didn't have to tell us any of that. We already knew; so he or she left that information out of their telling.

The point to remember is that even when outside folks are present, we tend to tell these family stories the same way we would if everyone were a family member. Without even thinking about it, we automatically omit all of the information from our stories that the *family* already knows and never notice that the outsiders are missing huge and critically important chunks of the story.

Your organization, your company, your department, your profession are all forms of "family." Each of these professional families builds up a tremendous amount of commonly held information (jargon, concepts, histories, definitions, acronyms, research, experiences, relationships, etc.). Well-functioning organizations actually require these organization-specific Banks of Prior Knowledge to exist. Miscommunications and mistakes would reign supreme without them.

You speak and write to each other using these communications shortcuts because they work and they are efficient. Everything is perfectly clear. You soon reach a point where you don't even notice that you do it.

Here's what the research shows. When you go outside the family, you still tend to talk and to write as you would to a family member. You forget that the audiences you face do not share in the Banks of Prior Knowledge that are, so often, the key underpinnings of the points you want to make. You forget because you are so used to communicating with people who *are* part of the family.

Family Stories: Once you get used to telling (communicating) to the family, you tend to tell (communicate) to everyone as if they were part of the family (and hold the family's common prior knowledge).

However, that forces your audience to kick their NSN and their Banks of Prior Knowledge into overdrive to fill in the gaps with what makes sense to them. Research experiments consistently identify two problems with that: 1) they are virtually always wrong with what they create and 2) their version is almost always more negative toward your organization, character, and information than you intended.

■ ■ ■

THE CURSE OF KNOWLEDGE

Let me introduce the *Curse of Knowledge:*

> *Once you <u>know</u>, it is impossible to accurately remember what it was like to <u>not know</u>.*

It has been demonstrated in lab and university research over and over. Once you have been part of the organization/work family long enough to know the field so well that you are in a position to be the one to communicate to outside groups, clients, funders, or other audiences, you know the material far too well to accurately envision what your audiences know and believe, to know how they view your field and your organization, to be able to look at your organization and material through their eyes.

Combine the Curse with the principle of family stories and we find:

> *Once you know, you tend to write and to speak as if <u>every</u> reader/listener also knows.*

The classic place the Curse rears its ugly head is in the language you use. Work language is almost always different from "weekend language" (the way you talk to family and neighbors at a Saturday block party barbecue or over the backyard fence). At work we spew jargon and acronyms. Why? Because at work—to *members of the work family*—that jargon forms an efficient shorthand language that works. It works at work.

Compare that to your weekend speech. On weekends we are typically conversational, simple, clear, and interesting. We stuff in more examples, details, emotional reactions, anecdotes, and analogies. It's not that your weekend speech is "good" and the work jargon is "bad." Both are effective if used only with the appropriate "family."

The Curse causes problem only when you think a set of words that creates a vivid and clear picture for you will do the same for everyone else—without thinking about whether they are part of that family. I was helping a class of fourth graders in a Pennsylvania school develop their ability to write details. I watched over one boy's shoulder as he wrote, "The dog went in the house." I could have gone after his verb and/or preposition choice. But I was working on writing details. So, I asked him to tell me more about the dog and about the house—maybe describe the front porch or the weather . . .

He stared at me as if I had to be the dumbest human being on earth. He then jabbed the point of his pencil at each word as he said (considerably louder than the first time), "The . . . dog . . . went . . . in . . . the . . . house!"

I said that I got that part but that I couldn't *see* the house or the dog in my mind unless he gave me more descriptive details. He sighed, rolled his eyes (as if I was truly beyond help and hope), and snapped, "I don't have to put any more in. I can already see it. It's my house and it's my dog!"

The curse of knowledge and family stories. It honestly never occurred to him that if the words he wrote popped a vivid picture into *his* mind, they wouldn't do the same for someone else. It turns out to be a complex mental gymnastics process to be able to see even a very small and simple slice of the world through someone else's eyes and mind. Neural researches call it theory of mind, that is, the ability to see the world from another's perspective; to empathize, to figuratively walk a mile in their shoes.

The Curse of Knowledge and the learned patterns of family stories make that feat considerably harder. Yet, it is critical to your successful communication. If you don't correctly anticipate and adjust your material for your audience, their Neural Story Net will still need to make it make sense, and they will use their own Banks of Prior Knowledge as the basis for the assumptions, interjections, guesses, and interpretations it makes in order to do so.

The greater the difference between the Banks of Prior Knowledge of the *communicator* (you) and of the *audience*, the greater the likelihood that your messages will suffer significant distortion—if they are not dumped onto the mental trash heap and ignored as making no sense and being too hard to interpret.

Write and speak from your audience's Banks of Prior Knowledge—not from yours, not from the experts', not from the organization's.

■ ■ ■

A FINAL CAUTION:
BOX BROWNIE MIX

A final caution: Just because you believe in your information, just because you can so clearly see its value, doesn't mean anyone else will—even after you show them.

A TV food show wanted to create the best-ever brownie recipe. As part of their testing, they took two brownies onto the streets of the city for public taste testing. One was a favorite made from scratch recipe. The other was a popular grocery store box mix. Passers-by sampled both brownies and then picked their favorite. The box mix won hands-down. Wasn't even close. Dumbfounded, the testers asked people why they chose that one. People answered that the box brownie reminded them of the brownies they ate as kids. They were familiar. They matched people's Banks of Prior Knowledge.

Just because you show people that your products, your information, your messages are better doesn't mean that they will like or accept them.

We tend to fight tenaciously to hold onto our existing Banks of Prior Knowledge—even when they are wrong, even when we are shown that they are wrong.

Brendon Nyhan (2014) at Dartmouth College just conducted a study of immunization messaging and found that it is much harder to change public opinion than previously thought. In a study of over 1,700 parents, they found that information about the safety of the MMR (measles, mumps, and rubella) vaccine made the parents believe in the safety of the vaccine. However—and this is the counterintuitive (and potentially disturbing) finding—those same parents who became more convinced of the vaccine's safety actually became less likely to want to vaccinate their children!

Nyhan concluded that when you are confronted by information you don't like, at one level you accept that the new information is true, yet—at a deeper level—you take it as an attack on your self-image and so fight back and rebel against this new information. Just as information alone will not fully engage an audience, so, too, it seems that information alone will not influence them. Engagement at an emotional level is required to overcome this natural resistance to new information.

In her book *The Story Factor* (2001), Annette Simmons writes (p. 3), "People value their own conclusions far more highly than yours . . ." It takes considerable energy and force to replace existing information in people's Banks of Prior Knowledge. Effective stories can provide that needed burst of energy.

"Stories anchor our beliefs. If you have a story, the only thing that changes your mind is a better story" (Taylor 1996, p. 71). I will again use this quote to open Part III, but it's worth using here as well.

Effective story structure can help. The human mind is programmed to be engaged by information presented in effective story structure, to pay attention to it. That gives you far better access to your audience's conscious minds and a better chance to influence (change beliefs, attitudes, values, knowledge, and behavior)—to change their Banks of Prior Knowledge.

To break past that defensive wall, inertial stories that are Powerful, Influential, and Effective will help. The rest of this book leads toward a system that will help you consistently create *those* stories.

This part of the book has laid out the case for using stories—describing what stories do, how the brain/mind of your intended audience processes information, and how stories can help you achieve your goals. With that build-up, two questions remain: 1) What are the elements of effective story structure, those informational elements human Neural Story Nets require in order to make sense? And 2) What is the most efficient and effective process for merging your themes, messages, and information with that effective story structure?

■ ■ ■

PART III

EIGHT ESSENTIAL ELEMENTS
OF STORY

WHAT IS A STORY?

We now arrive at the heart of effective stories. This is where the findings of neural science meet story structure and story design. The Eight Essential Elements we'll develop in this part are those elements that match the informational demands of your readers' and listeners' Neural Story Net as it struggles to make sense and to understand. Effective stories are those that supply what the NSN requires.

> Stories anchor our beliefs. If you have a story, the only thing that changes your mind is a better story. (Taylor, 1996, p. 220)

Said in a more scientific way, if you have Prior Knowledge (right or wrong) saved into memory in story form, the only thing that will compel you to change that existing belief is information in a replacement story that is more powerful, influential, and effective than the original.

While I deeply believe in the truth of that quote, and while the research also consistently supports it, it still begs the question: **What is a story?**

From previous sections, it is clear that story—at least what people call "effective story" or "good story"—is the root of all narrative forms and structures. First came stories; then came poems, plays, essays, lectures, monologues, articles, encyclopedia entries, and so on. Story is the quintessential base of human communications. That's how we are wired. That's how we are programmed to understand and to make sense. We are truly *Homo narratus*: story animals.

Effective stories *engage* audiences and hold that engagement (cause listeners to pay attention). That engagement is the essential gateway to *influence* (the alteration of beliefs, attitudes, values, knowledge, and behavior). Effective story structure is the delivery vehicle. Your imbedded thematic messages and images are the payload. Story structure opens the mind and memory of the receiver, paving the way for the successful delivery of that payload message, information, teaching, or image.

I have studied over 1,000 research findings, articles, and books from 16 separate fields of related study and research. What do they collectively conclude? Overwhelmingly, the research shows that effective story architecture (the assembled structural—informational—elements of effective story structure):

- Provides superior retention (memory and recall)
- Provides improved understanding
- Creates context and relevance
- Creates empathy
- Provides superior engagement
- Better induces listeners/readers to pay attention
- Enhances the creation of meaning

That's an impressive list. Dozens—often hundreds—of references from prominent research scientists back up every item on that list. Note that the list is exactly what you want from your communications.

At this point in workshops, I often flash up a slide that says:

> *There are only three rules for creating great stories . . .*

Everyone grabs paper and pen, ready to write—until I shift slides to:

> *There are only three rules for creating great stories . . .*
> *Unfortunately, nobody knows what any of them are.*

Everyone chuckles. But, deep down, most of us have a gut-level feeling that it's true. Name a rule for writing narrative stories—any rule: "Stories should be written in past tense . . . or in third person . . . or in complete sentences . . . or with words correctly spelled . . . or with standard punctuation conventions." Go ahead. Name any rule. Then go down to your public library, and librarians there will be able to easily pull award-winning stories off of the shelves that intentionally violate any rule you can name.

That's because we look for the wrong kind of rules. Those rules are like highway speed limits are rules. That kind of rule was created specifically to be violated. We need to look for a wholly different kind of rule.

We need to find a story rule more like *gravity* is a rule for the physical universe. Now there's a **rule**! You can't wake up late and speed your drive to work by shifting your car to half-grav. You can't cheat gravity when you step on the scale in order to get the number you want. Gravity is. Period.

Then along came Newton. In junior high school I believed that Newton *invented* gravity. Turns out that's wrong. Scientists whose names we never learned had known about gravity in detail for centuries before Newton's time. What Newton did was give us the *rules* for describing gravity. For that gift, we have set Newton on a pedestal so high that in 1970 when American astronomer Vera Rubin became the first human to measure the velocity of individual stars in distant galaxies and found that none of them travelled through space at the speed Newton's equations predicted, she was told that she was not allowed to suggest that Newton was wrong. In searching for another explanation, she created the idea of *dark matter*.

Dark matter is this "stuff" we cannot see, hear, smell, or touch. We cannot detect in any way. Why do we know dark matter is there? Because without it, Newton's equations don't work. Stop and ponder that amazing concept for a moment. We'd rather believe in this invisible, undetectable "stuff" than even suggest the *possibility* that Newton was wrong. Now *that* is putting someone on a pedestal!

That's **rules**! That's the kind of rules we're looking for to help us describe the elements that comprise the structure of effective stories.

However, that again loops us back to the basic question: What is a story?

In a more practical sense, what is it that makes a story stick? What makes us gravitate toward good stories? What makes us pay such close attention? What makes them vividly stick for years in our memories? What makes stories so much stickier than other forms of narrative?

Time for you to go to work. Write down your definition for a story. Definitions, of course, are how we both differentiate one thing from all other things and characterize that one thing we are defining. The best definitions do both. What words would you use to define a story? I have found in workshops that it is very valuable to have people pause to struggle over the language they would use for their definition of story.

Please, take the time to grab a piece of paper and write *your* definition before you go on. Try to be as specific and precise as you can.

Was it hard to select specific language to use? Are you satisfied that your definition clearly identifies what makes "good" stories so alluring, engaging, powerful, and effective? Did your definition differentiate story from other forms of narrative? Effective definitions give us clear guidance and direction. Does yours?

HINT

A brief aside to share with you the best editing trick you will ever have. Read what you write out loud to another person. Immediate family and really good friends don't count. Neither does it count to read it to yourself. (When you read your own writing to yourself, you *always* think it is wonderful.) Sit knee-to-knee, eye-to-eye and read to some other person what you have written.

The other person will not do a thing other than sit and listen. You, however, will watch very closely how *you* react as you read. If you find yourself wanting to pause and explain, or to add a quick aside, don't do it. It means that you aren't satisfied with what you wrote. Don't pause to take notes. Just keep reading. But do make a vertical mark in the margin next to those lines. Your displeasure is politely telling yourself you'll need to do a bit of rewriting.

If you find yourself looking forward to a part that is coming up, you are actually telling yourself that you don't like the part you are reading. Mark in the margin. If you find yourself speeding up, growing softer, and so on, you are always saying that you don't like the lines you are reading. If you develop the urge to stop and say, "We'll stop here. I'll rewrite that first part. Then we'll try again." You are really saying that you hate the part that is just ahead. Mark it and keep reading. You'll find that you quite accurately identify everything you aren't satisfied with about the piece you wrote.

Try it. Read your definition out loud to another person. Try to pretend that you love this definition and are sure you are exactly right. How did it sound? Want to revise it? Rethink it? Add to it? "Borrow" something you heard someone else say when they read their definition and stuff it onto yours?

Try it. Stop here and actually revise and rewrite your definition.

Look at concepts you used. Did you define what a story *is*, or did you identify the *effect* you want a story to have on a receiver? (That would be more a characteristic than a definition and begs the question: What is it about a story that does that?)

Most attendees in my workshops define a story from the viewpoint of the *listener* and describe what they feel when they hear a good story. That approach makes sense, since most of your experience is as the story receiver. Unfortunately, defining story from the listener's vantage point won't help you or guide you as the teller.

My point: We are all hardwired to automatically think and perceive in specific story terms. Yet, as a culture (and to our detriment) we allow ourselves to be overly vague in our conscious understanding of story and too lax in the specificity with which we describe this most powerful of communications tools.

Let me change tacks and come at the definition another way. What do you think is the difference between a story and:

> A magazine article?
>
> An essay?
>
> An encyclopedia entry?
>
> A memo?
>
> A picnic spread out over an unseen anthill?
>
> A recipe?
>
> A basketball game play-by-play report?
>
> A poem?
>
> A directive?
>
> A conversation?
>
> Last summer?
>
> A newspaper column?
>
> A joke?

Are these all stories? Do they all *make* stories? Are *some* stories? Surely, they do not *all* match what we mean when we say "story"! Is there overlap, then, between story and these other narrative forms? What makes some articles stories and some not? What makes some jokes stories and some not? When is an essay a story and when is it not? What *is* a story?

Let's try to approach "story" from yet one more angle. Do you think that the following people are all referring to the same thing—even though they all use the same word: "story"?

- An editor growls, "What's the story?" to a cub reporter.
- A drama critic searches for a movie's "dramatic story arc."
- A therapist asks a patient to recount a rambling series of life events.
- A second grade teacher asks her students for a half-page story about a dragon.
- A minister begins a recitation of a biblical parable.
- A father barks, "Don't you tell *me* your wild stories!" to a son who came home three hours after curfew.
- A grizzled detective flips open his notebook and licks his pencil stub as he arrives at the crime scene and growls to the rookie cop who discovered the body, "So, what's the story?"
- A food critic writes a book on the history and cultivation of the carrot.
- A man drifts across a crowded cocktail party, pauses next to a woman who picks at the shrimp platter, and says, "So, what's your story?"
- A couple shares the events of the day over dinner.
- A daughter snuggled into bed pleads, "Tell me a story!" to her mother.

Do they all mean the same thing when they use the word "story" to describe what they are doing? The answer, of course, is no. But what does that say for your definition of what is and what is not a story? How do you separate the stories from the nonstories?

Those questions are often hard to answer because most people confuse content with story. The word "story" does not directly refer to the content (the information). Rather:

"Story" refers to how that content is organized.

The Eight Essential Elements define that effective story organization and structure.

Any of the items in the previous two lists could be put in effective story form by building the story around those eight elements. They could each also be taken out of that effective story form. Organizing material into effective story form is all about organizing it around those informational elements that the receiver's Neural Story Net (NSN) requires in order to make sense and to understand without imposing excessive distortion or alteration to that information so that the resulting conscious mental construct of the story accurately matches your original version and imagery. That is the linkage between brain and story.

Story is the delivery vehicle that carries your information to the conscious mind of the listener. It is the booster rocket that aims and delivers your payload. It is . . . well, you get the idea. The form and organization of effective stories guide the NSN in its work to interpret and to create meaning.

Thus, "story" is as much a way of thinking, planning, and approaching how you'll shape your material as it is the final physical thing—the story—itself. Story thinking guides you to plan the elements of what you'll write or say by first considering how they'll be heard and how your audience will make sense of them.

Once again, we are back to the basic question: What is a story? What are the specific elements that uniquely define effective story structure?

If you want a definition, where do you go? If you're over 50, it's the dictionary. If you are younger, your answer is probably "Wikipedia."

I have looked up "story" in eight English dictionaries and online. While many of these sources list more than 20 possible meanings for "story," every one of them as their primary definition uses either these exact words or words that have the exact same meaning.

story, n: A narrative account of a real or imagined event or events.

Do you accept that definition? Does that adequately identify what you mean when you say "story"? Does that uniquely describe what you seek and hope to use?

Since my background lies in science, let's test it. Imagine this scene: You are a parent of a fifth grade boy who storms into the house after school, slams down his book bag, and says, "My teacher is so unfair! She's making us write a story tonight and turn it in tomorrow." After three hours of working on his story, he slides a piece of paper onto the kitchen table, crosses his arms, and announces, "*There* is my story."

You pick up the piece of paper. On it is written,

He went to the store.

Did he, or did he not, write a story? Yes or no?

If you say, "Yes, it fits with the dictionary definition," is that really what you mean when you say "story"? Is that what you are after? Stories stick. They get remembered. They engage and influence. They hold our rapt attention. That one-line narrative does none of those things.

If you say, "No, he didn't," glance back at the dictionary definition. Isn't the boy's line of text a "narrative account of a real or imagined event"?

Conclusion: The dictionary is wrong.

It's actually an irony of English. English, the largest language on Earth at well over 1 million words, has an incredible dearth of vocabulary to describe narrative forms of the language. Russian has more. German has more. I am told that Chinese has more. English has no word for the opposite of story (for "not story").

We tend to define concepts by creating words for binary opposites (black—white, good—evil, tall—short, etc.). Then we fill in with a multitude of other words to express gradations along that scale. Rather than admit the lack of a "not-story" word, dictionaries chose to stretch the one word they had—"story"—to cover everything.

It is much like the situation we'd have if we had only one word to describe precipitation. Someone steps in from outside and shakes out his coat, splattering droplets across the room. You ask, "What's going on out there?" He answers, "Precipitation." It's suddenly laughable. Think of how many words English offers to describe different temperatures of precipitation, different densities of precipitation, different volumes and velocities of precipitation. Yet English offers no counterword to "story" in common usage to describe other narrative structures.

Big mistake. It's made the word "story" virtually meaningless in common usage. Everything, in common usage, becomes a story. (Including, "He went to the store.") The word "story" becomes meaningless, and all differential meaning must be transferred to modifiers (**good** story, **boring** story, **effective** story, **powerful** story . . .)

Let's cut through the definitional fog and make it simple. We want to define *good stories*—effective stories, stories that stick, stories you want to craft and use as centerpieces of your communications. To do that, we must abandon the dictionary's one-word-fits-all definition and narrow our focus onto that subset of stories that *are* described as "effective stories." For our purposes, the word "story" now equals "effective story." We need to isolate and characterize those stories that are effective in accomplishing their mission, and we want our definition to identify the elements that separates those stories from narratives that are not as effective. We seek a definition that will serve as a reliable guide to constructing, planning, crafting, editing, molding, and adapting consistently effective stories.

I have approached a definition for this meaning of story in three independent ways over the last 30 years. The first was as a storyteller who wrote all of my own performance stories. Through thousands of on-stage performances, I tweaked, modified, and adjusted my stories, trying to identify the essential elements that held audience engagement and made them want to listen to more stories. Over a couple of decades, I honed in on eight specific elements that consistently controlled audience response.

The second was through my research that was launched by the NASA challenge mentioned earlier. Over the course of more than two years, I read and compared over 700 reports, articles, white papers, and books from the most prominent researchers in 16 fields of neural, cognitive, psychological, biological, and informational sciences. When I synthesized all of this research (the vast majority of which was conducted with absolutely no thought or concern for stories), I found the same eight elements.

The final approach came through a DARPA (the science research arm of the Department of Defense) research program that was looking into the neuroscience of story with a particular focus on understanding how stories exert influence. Here

I was able to start from the other end: What happens inside the mind of a story receiver? How is the human brain wired and programmed to make sense, to understand, remember and recall? With access to a modern EEG lab, I was able to use modern neural and cognitive science to build a model of how we humans process incoming story information. I was able to create test stories and then variations on those stories that would isolate and shift individual elements or combinations of elements. I told different versions to different audiences and, using the brain activity scans, measured the effect of altering different aspects of a story.

Once again, I arrived at the same eight informational elements as being the key controllers and drivers of how audiences understand, make sense of, and visualize a story. The same eight elements. But this time, I arrived at this conclusion by watching the demands of audience members' Neural Story Net (NSN). These Eight Essential Elements *are* essential specifically because they match the informational demands of the NSN.

My conclusion is that these Eight Essential Elements:

1. Uniquely define the structure of effective stories
2. Exactly match the informational demands of the human Neural Story Net
3. Are the principle informational drivers of the Make Sense Mandate
4. Define what every researcher means when they say that humans learn and think in story terms and through stories.

■ ■ ■

—— THE EIGHT ESSENTIAL ELEMENTS ——

It's time to ask the question: What are those Eight Essential Elements?

I'll list them first and then put them through their paces one by one to show you what each contributes to reader/listener perception and understanding.

The Eight Essential Elements of the Story Structure

1. **Characters:**	The characters that populate essential character positions in the story.
2. **Traits:**	Selected elements of character description used to control receiver attitude toward, and relationship to, story characters.
3. **Goal:**	What a character needs/wants to do/get in a story.
4. **Motives:**	The sets of drivers that make a goal important to a character. Goals and motives are the primary source of story suspense.
5. **Conflicts and problems:**	The sets of obstacles that stand between a character and an established goal and block that character from reaching the goal.
6. **Risk and danger:**	The likelihood of failure (risk) and the consequences of failure (danger) created by problems and conflicts that a character must face. Risk and danger are the primary source of story excitement. Excitement and suspense are the primary sources of **story tension**.
7. **Struggles:**	The sequence of events a character undertakes (struggles) to reach a goal highlighted by the climax scene (confrontation with the last and greatest obstacle) and the resolution scene.
8. **Details:**	The character-, sensory-, scenic-, and event-specific descriptors used to create, direct, and control receivers' story imagery.

In sentence form, an effective story consists of

> a **character** that is of **interest** to the intended audience has a **goal** that is both important to that character (**motive**) and relevant to the audience. However, reaching that goal is blocked by some combination of **problems and conflicts** that create real **risk and danger** for the main character. Still, this main character **struggles** to overcome problems and conflicts, facing risk and danger, to achieve that important goal. This story must, then, be presented in sufficient relevant **detail** to make it seem real, vivid, and compelling.

Those are the elements of effective stories: stories that engage and hold audience attention. Now let's see what each contributes to an effective story.

☐ ☐ *Let's go back to that fifth grader's story.*

He went to the store.

We want to turn that one boring sentence into a *good* story, an *effective* story, a memorable and powerful story—into what many would call a **real** story. What information do you want to know and add in order to do that? Actually, what everyone requests are the Eight Essential Elements, though they might use different wording when making those informational requests.

The Eight Essential Elements are numbered (elements 1 through 8) in that specific order because creating them in that order consistently proves to be the most effective and efficient sequence for the development of effective stories.

However, we'll skip around a bit in the numerical order of the elements for this developmental demonstration so as to build a clear picture of what each element is and what it contributes to our developing story.

Let's take those requests for information one at a time, beginning with the one most frequently requested by audiences during my workshops. Then we will work our way through all eight of the essential elements.

The first request usually mentioned is, "*Why* did he go to the store?" We'll start there, even though that pulls us straight to element 3.

Note that the word "he" in our sentence suggests a character (elements 1 and 2). So, most people skip over those two linked elements and save the question of who *he* is for later.

■ ■ ■

ELEMENT 3: GOAL

Easily 95 percent of the time the first question asked is, "*Why* did he go to the store?"

The informational element you seek is a goal. We have at least identified a character ("he"), even though we know nothing about him. In order to have this make any sense, we need to know what he's after. We need to know his goal.

By definition:

Goal: What a character needs or wants to do or get in a story

It is not what they do; not what they actually accomplish. It is what they are after, what drives them. This one critical element of story information also allows readers to understand the point, purpose, and structure of the story.

A quick demonstration of the incredible power of an explicit goal:

Once there was a girl named Mary who wanted some ice cream.

There, in one sentence, are a character and her goal. Now you tell me: How will this story end? What will happen at the very end of this story? Answer the questions yourself. Ask as many others as you like, and you will find that every answer is some variant of either she gets her ice cream or she doesn't get it.

*** Stories end when the primary goal of the main character is resolved, one way or another.***

I could now go on with that story for an hour and—somehow—have her scrambling up Mt. Kilimanjaro just minutes ahead of bloodthirsty pirates and slave traders. In the back of your mind, you would be thinking, "Ooooow, this isn't going to help her get that ice cream. This is making it harder for her to get her ice cream!"

From neurophysicist R. Montague (2006, p. 48): "Remarkably, the single property that all biological and mechanical computational systems require is goals."

Famed researcher Pinker (1997) agrees that beliefs and goals drive behavior. But Pinker goes further, showing that if we are to truly understand behavior, we must first understand beliefs and goals.

Every action and event in a story is interpreted by receivers based on its impact on a character's ability to achieve goal.

Writer Lisa Cron (2012, p. 14) says, "We are always looking for the 'why' question to answer, 'What does it mean?' " The "why" question is answered by a goal.

Goal is a hugely important element of story information. Goal establishes the point and purpose of a story for the receiver's Neural Story Net. It creates the basic framework of story structure. With no goal, there's no way to establish personal relevance and meaning; no way to get listeners to become deeply and personally invested in the characters and in the story; no way to get excited about, or to understand, story actions and events.

Here is another demonstration of the power and importance of concrete goals. Read the following paragraph. Does it make sense? Do you understand it?

> *Sally let loose a team of gophers. The plan backfired when a dog chased them away. She then threw a party, but the guests failed to bring their motorcycles. Furthermore, her stereo system was not loud enough. Sally spent the next day looking for an obnoxiously loud squawking parrot but was unable to find one in the Yellow Pages. Nonstop sales calls gave her some hope until the number was changed. It was the installation of a blinking neon light across the street that finally did the trick. Sally framed the ad for the light from the classified section and now has it hanging on her wall.*

Almost everyone who reads this paragraph answers that no, they don't have any idea what this paragraph is really about or what is going on here.

This paragraph is pure plot: action. Notice that plot and action do not hook you into the story. They do not create excitement. They do not establish the point and purpose of the story. Plot (the sequence of events) is cheap. It's dime-a-dozen stuff. Lay out and design your story with the Eight Essential Elements. *Then* worry about plot.

If I want you to understand this paragraph about Sally, all I have to do is add a goal for her. That goal will instantly create point and purpose to every action. Goal gives you a way to evaluate and to understand each action and event. Goal creates meaning for events.

> *Sally hates the woman who moved in next door and* **wants to drive her out.**

There is a goal statement for Sally: what she wants to do. Reread the paragraph and see if it now makes sense. You may disagree with Sally's tactics. However, with a goal in hand, you fully understand them.

> *Sally let loose a team of gophers. The plan backfired when a dog chased them away. She then threw a party, but the guests failed to bring their motorcycles. Furthermore, her stereo system was not loud enough. Sally spent the next day looking for an obnoxiously loud squawking parrot but was unable to find one in the Yellow Pages. Nonstop sales calls gave her some hope until the number was changed. It was the installation of a blinking neon light across the street that finally did the trick. Sally framed the ad for the light from the classified section and now has it hanging on her wall.*

That is the power of a goal. Yet, it is amazing how many people skip over goal in presenting their stories and jump straight to the action. I suspect it is an example of the curse of knowledge in full swing. You live with the struggle to reach your goals every day. You know them so well, you forget others need to hear them in order to understand your story. It's an example of the Curse of Knowledge in action. You know your own goals so well and so deeply that you forget that others can't see them as soon as you begin your presentation or written piece.

What makes this trend more insidious is that story authors learned many years ago the value of implying key character goals. Those authors, however, have learned the art and skill of leaving an unmistakable trail of breadcrumb clues for readers to follow. The bottom line is that many authors don't overtly state character goals; we get used to not seeing them in print, and we forget that we must find a way to make the goals of main characters clear to our audiences.

Goldilocks is an excellent example. You know the story of young Goldilocks. In the opening paragraph she commits a felony as she breaks into and enters the bears' house. If she's caught, she's looking at hard time in the slammer! Why did she do it? Why'd she go in there and risk jail or death by bear claw? What was her goal?

Most readers pick up on the risk and danger (bears) and charge on with the action as Goldi wanders the house, gobbles porridge, and wrecks furniture. It is thereby relegated to a "cute story for four- and five-year-olds."

But consider the power in this story that lies dormant waiting for an assigned goal that is important to the character and relevant to some target audience. The following were suggested as goal and motive for Goldilocks by an eighth grade class during a workshop of mine in 2004:

1. Goldilocks picked the bears' house instead of the sweet deer's house or the cute bunny's house because she has been bullied at school and wants to commit suicide.
2. Goldilocks wants to join a gang and must commit a dangerous felony before she can be considered for admission.
3. Goldilocks wants to steal back Grandma's secret recipe for perfect porridge that the bears stole from Granny so that Granny can win the porridge-making contest at the county fair and get the prize money that will pay for Grandpa's needed heart operation.
4. It's revenge! The bears ate Grandpa. Goldilocks doesn't yet know how she'll do it, but she's broken in to get even somehow.

I am not advocating the suicidal version of Goldilocks. But if you tell the story of Goldilocks at a middle or high school and make it clear that that's why she decided to bust into the bears' house, your audience will hang on every word to find out how that goal resolves at story's end. That's the power of a goal that is important to the character and relevant to the audience.

That's the power you unleash when you create main character goals that are important to the character and relevant to your intended audience—and then be sure you have made those goals clear to your audiences in your story presentation.

One final note on goals. Effective goals are physical and tangible. Nonspecific, nontangible concepts (happiness, peace, success, etc.) make poor story goals. Readers can't visualize what such goals looks like and so have no way to evaluate whether a character is getting closer. Keep your goals physical and tangible and let those nontangibles serve as motive. (We'll get to motive—element 4—in a bit.)

☐ ☐ *Back to the story we're trying to build.*

We started with "He went to the store." Unacceptably boring. We need to add element 3: **a** *goal* for "He went to the store." Here's one:

> He went to the store **for some milk**.
> He got some.
>
> The end.

There is our goal. Is the story now satisfying? Engaging? No. Goal sets the story framework in place but does not—by itself—create a story. Goal resolution (what we have here) ends the story but is not the story itself.

■ ■ ■

ELEMENT 5: CONFLICTS AND PROBLEMS

Stories happen *on the way* to resolving goals. Once you reach goal resolution, the story is over. That means that something must initially be keeping every character from reaching his or her goal. If nothing blocks them, they would already have achieved their goal.

There are only two things that can block a character from reaching a goal: problems and conflicts.

1. PROBLEMS. Most dictionaries cast a wide net with their definitions of "problem":

- A matter or situation needing to be dealt with and overcome
- A situation, matter, or person that presents perplexity or difficulty
- Something that is difficult to deal with; something that is a source of trouble, worry, etc.

For our purposes of building the framework of effective stories, we can tighten that definition a bit to focus on the role of problems in helping a reader's NSN make sense of your material.

> Problem: **A problem is *anything* that blocks a character (even temporarily) from reaching a goal.**

Story problems serve the story by acting as obstacles blocking a character from a stated goal. Problems that do not block a character from a goal can serve as interesting character traits. In long stories (novels) they can act to flesh out characters and make them more complex for readers. You, however, aren't writing novels. You need to focus you thinking on problems that serve as obstacles.

2. CONFLICT. Dictionaries define "conflict" as:

- A serious disagreement or argument
- Strong disagreement between people, groups, etc.
- A fight, battle, or struggle, especially a prolonged struggle; strife; controversy; quarrel: *conflicts between parties*

Conflict involves **characters in opposition**. It is that direct opposition between characters that is the focus of most stories. For our purpose of developing and defining effective stories, we can define conflict as:

> Conflict: **A conflict is a problem that places a character in direct opposition to some character or entity in a story.**

Yes, story conflict can (and routinely does) include fights with the character him- or herself. After all, the best fighting is always against yourself. Don't we all struggle to resolve conflicts between competing goals, needs, and loyalties? Those are very real forms of internal conflict.

"Problem" is the general catchall term. "Conflict" is a specific subset of problems. Every conflict is a problem. Many problems do not create conflict. Having five miles to walk to reach your car, for example, is a problem. (It temporarily blocks you from reaching your goal.) It is a problem, but it doesn't spawn any conflict.

We separate conflict into its own pullout category because of the markedly different affect conflicts have on story receivers.

I have found that many organizations, companies, and—especially—military commands are loath to even acknowledge the existence of problems and conflicts, and they are far more reticent to feature them in their stories. If it makes the concept easier to swallow, think of them as "challenges," as "obstacles" to overcome, even as "opportunities."

Many—if not most—nonprofit organizations form because of, and expressly to combat, some existing problem: cancer, poverty, discrimination, and so on. These uber-issues serve best as motive, explaining why we do what we do. Stories come alive with specifics. The specific problems and conflicts an individual story character (patient, researcher, community organizer, etc.) must deal with in order to succeed in their personal struggle. Those specific problems and conflicts are the more effective focus of your stories.

At a more basic level, there is nothing worthwhile that either you or your organization have ever accomplished that did not involve the struggle to overcome obstacles and challenges. If there was effort involved in accomplishing something, then it is always true that that effort was expended overcoming obstacles to success.

No problems, no conflicts: no story. Period.

If the thing you want to talk about was so easy to do that it required no exerted effort, if you had no obstacles to overcome—if it was truly that trivial—then why are you telling us about it? If you do, it will sound like bragging and will repel, not engage, your audience.

Will any problems do? No. For the story to make sense, the problems you include must serve as obstacles that block (even temporarily) a character from resolving a goal.

An example: Bob was uncomfortably nervous in front of crowds and hated giving speeches. He had also run out of toothpaste, hadn't been able to brush this morning, and thought he might have onion breath. There are three potential problems.

However, if the next line is: "Today, however, Bob was on vacation in his Arctic cabin and wouldn't see another human for two weeks," you instantly lose interest in the toothpaste and speech making. They don't matter. They won't get in Bob's way. They won't create any problems for him. At best, those descriptive bits will be relegated to character traits that make Bob a bit more interesting. However, they will clearly not drive and define this story.

However, if a hungry polar bear that loves onions wanders through, sniffing the air, the toothpaste bit is back front and center in our minds. It is now a dangerous problem that could easily block Bob from his goals: enjoy his vacation, live past today, and so on.

The hardwiring of your NSN seeks obstacles that stand in the path of goal resolution. Including problems that don't serve that function forces listeners' NSNs to either invent a connection that could make the problem relevant or partially pull out of the story to ponder whether they need to hold onto these asides or if they can disregard the story in its entirety.

Finally, notice that without an established goal, the problems and conflicts you mention cannot hope to create engagement, excitement, or involvement. Why? Problems are relevant within a story structure only when they serve as obstacles between character and goal.

Two examples will show you both the allure and the necessity of problems.

A Telling Example	*The Lone Ranger sat in his room polishing spurs and silver bullets when he heard someone cry, "Help! The bank is being robbed!"* *The Lone Ranger (LR for short) buckled his gun belt, tied on his mask, checked his dazzling white smile in the mirror, and raced downstairs and out onto the town's one main dirt street. There he found blind, crippled, 88-year-old Swedley Sweet hobbling from the bank leaning heavily on his cane, holding one shiny penny, and muttering, "Ha! I'm a rich man now . . ."* *The Ranger dashed across the street, scooped Swedly up, tucked him under one uniformed arm, carried him to the sheriff's office, and flung him into a cell. Brushing dust off of his gloves, LR smiled his triumphant smile and announced, "Another crime solved! He's in here for life."*

Did you identify with the Lone Ranger during this story? Were you rooting for him? Did you feel as if you were right there with him? Did you feel a rush of glowing satisfaction at his successful goal resolution? Were you fully engaged, wanting to find out what happened to Lone?

No. He comes across as an arrogant bully. You are far more likely to side with Swedley, to sympathize with him, to empathize with him. If this were a law-and-order video story, it would backfire horribly. The cops come across as the bad guys. But why? LR was upholding the law and making a dutiful arrest.

Research has shown that a core value of all Western civilizations is a sense of fairness. It is a core part of our sense of right and wrong that lies at the heart of our Banks of Prior Knowledge.

The solution for this story problem is . . . problems. We need to create problems and conflicts for LR to overcome.

A Telling Example	*At the cry "Help! The bank's being robbed!" Mr. Ranger raced downstairs so fast, he forgot to grab his boots and gun belt. As he hobbles onto the street in his stocking feet, he finds not only Swedly (who carries a sack stuffed with every penny owned by the goodly townsfolk) but also his gang of fifteen heavily armed thugs. The thugs grab LR, wrap him up in barbed wire, and toss him onto the train tracks thirty seconds ahead of the speeding 2:10 on its way to Yuma as they laugh and say that if the train doesn't get him, the dynamite they buried around town will vaporize the whole place in five minutes.*

Now we have a story. With only a busted pocket comb for a weapon, LR has to escape the barbed wire, dodge the train, defuse the dynamite, fight off the thugs—all in order to arrest Swedley and save the town. Now you are rooting for the Ranger. Now you are on his side. Now you are engaged.

No problems, no conflicts: no story.

That's the power of featuring problems and conflicts in your story. They allow characters to valiantly and nobly struggle as they allow audiences to become engaged, to identify with those characters, and thereby to adopt the character's perspective, attitude, and values (i.e., to be influenced).

☐ ☐ ***Back to the story we're trying to build.***

We started with "He went to the store." Unacceptably boring. We added a goal. Now we need to add element 5: *problems and conflicts* for "He went to the store." Since conflicts are more powerful and appealing to audiences (I'll explain why when we get to the next element), we'll create a conflict for "He" to face. Here's one:

> *He went to the store for some milk.*
> **But a golden butterfly perched on the door handle,**
> **twitched its wings, and hissed, "You can't come in!"**
> *He brushed away the butterfly, walked into the store,*
> *and got his milk.*
>
> *The end.*

There is a conflict. Our main character is placed in direct opposition to another. The butterfly does represent an obstacle that blocks (albeit very temporarily) our character from reaching his goal.

But is it exciting? Is it engaging? Do you care about "He" and his milk?

No. It's the same problem the Lone Ranger faced. We need more than just problems and conflicts if we are to make the story exciting and engaging.

■ ■ ■

—— ELEMENT 6: RISK AND DANGER ——

Here is a question to ponder. Why don't you care about the story with a lone but-terfly as the conflict character (the enemy, the antagonist) for our main character? More importantly, what must I add to make you begin to care?

The answer is Risk and Danger. Again, let's start by defining our terms.

> **Risk:** The probability of failure; the likelihood that something will go wrong
>
> **Danger:** The consequences of failure; what happens if something does go wrong

Risk and danger are the drivers of excitement, tension, and drama. The risks and dangers that accomplish that heroic feat are created for the main character by the problems and conflicts he will have to face and struggle to overcome.

Because risk is essentially zero for "He" confronting a lone butterfly, we don't care. You likely didn't even bother to consider whether there was any danger. It is as if the story excitement factor (some researchers call it jeopardy) is the mathematical product of risk times danger. If risk = 0, it doesn't matter what danger is, the prod-uct is still a boring zero.

Risk and danger are what lock us into a story and make us need to find out what happens. Risk and danger make your characters compelling and sympathetic. They make story readers want to identify with your characters. Said in gambling terms, if a player puts nothing on the table, how can we possibly care about what cards she is dealt?

As part of normal daily existence, we continuously scan for potential risk and dan-ger. Why do you look both ways before crossing the street? Because it drastically reduces risk (the likelihood that you'll be flattened by a speeding semi). Looking both ways doesn't reduce danger (what happens to you if you *are* hit by that semi), but it almost eliminates risk. Why do teens want to know about how deep the water is before they willingly jump off of a 30-foot tower into a lake? Knowing that there are no jagged rocks (or hungry piranha) reduces danger.

In virtually every moment and situation we, like a radar station on a navy ship, probe the surrounding waters, performing risk and danger assessments. Every audience member's brain is used to working with risk and danger information. Your Neural Story Net requires it in order to evaluate individual events, the story in general, and—more importantly—your characters.

Consider this example. Picture an empty basketball gym floor. Now place a 40-foot-long four-by-four wooden post on the floor. Would you be willing to walk the entire length of that four-by-four for $50? Probably yes. Would you be willing to sit in the bleachers and pay $50 to watch someone else walk the four-by-four? Most probably not.

Yet, if I want to make you willing to pay that $50, I do not need to change the action—walk the length of the four-by-four. It is never the action itself that makes audiences willing to pay with either their money or their attention. All I have to do is increase the risk and danger.

I won't place the four-by-four on the floor. I'll suspend it 1,000 feet in the air, over a craggy cliff and shark-infested waters (increased danger—what happens to my volunteer if he falls?). Then I'll wait for a hurricane to roar up the coast so that the winds aloft are blowing at 120 miles per hour and the four-by-four vibrates like a violin string as it sways back and forth (increased risk—the likelihood my volunteer will fall).

Now if I could find someone willing to climb up a 1,000-foot-high rope ladder and walk across that four-by-four, you know that I could fill a stadium of eager watchers who would gladly pay $50 for the cheap seats. The only thing that would make the crowd boo and demand a refund would be for my daredevil to chicken out and refuse to climb all the way up to face the risk and danger.

A vibrant industry of stunt people has grown up in this country to take advantage for our lust to watch others face risk and danger. Evil Knievel is not the only one to earn millions for a single wild stunt. Is there really any valuable life learning in knowing how many flaming school busses you can jump over on your motorcycle? Certainly not. Still, every few years someone new adds another bus to the row and takes a run at it.

Why flaming busses? Extra danger. Why more and more of them to jump over? Greater risk.

> Excitement = Risk times Danger
> Tension = Excitement plus Suspense

According to the common saying: *As goes tension, so goes attention!*

Everything you do that is worth doing and worth reporting to your audiences required you to face considerable risk and danger: risk of failure, of embarrassment, of ridicule, of rejection, of abandonment, of losing your job, of losing your self-image and self-worth, of destitution, of losing your self-respect, of reaching the wrong conclusion, of making an error, and so on. Notice that I have not yet included any physical dangers. Physical ones are fine—especially for movies—but it is the personal, social, mental, and emotional dangers that will truly resonate with your audiences.

What kind of risks and dangers? Embarrassment, rejection, ridicule, belittlement, being laughed at, being abandoned, being scorned, being unwanted, failure, lack of results, fears, and so on and so on.

Consider this potential story: A 14-year-old boy, Bob, is determined to dance with Sally at the school sock hop later this afternoon. That's a character and goal. If I want to fully engage you in this story, I must create a compelling collection of problems and conflicts for Bob to face.

Bob's best friend bets Bob $5 that Bob won't dare to even ask Sally, let alone actually dance with her. Bob accepts the bet. Word spreads through the class. Soon nine other boys have each made the same $5 bet with Bob. By lunch Bob is shocked to realize that he has bet $50 he doesn't have. He can't pay if he loses his bets, so he must go through with it.

At lunch Carol, a friend of Bob's, tells him that the girls also know about his bet and that Sally said she would rather passionately kiss a moldy, wart-covered toad than get within 10 feet of Bob.

Sock hop time. Everyone knows. All the boys wait on one side of the gym. All the girls wait on the other. All are watching Bob. He can't get out of it. As 500 faces stare and giggle, he starts his long tortured walk across the gym floor toward Sally to face total humiliation. Nervous sweat dribbles down his face and spreads as a huge stain from his armpits. As he practices his line, his voice (for the first time) begins to break and squeak. A huge zit pops out on the end of his nose. Bob can't make his feet turn back and save him from this life-shattering disaster . . .

And now you want to know what will happen. Don't you? That's the power of social and emotional risk and danger.

Featuring—even emphasizing—the risk and danger your company, organization, department, or self have and do face is **STORY SMART** storytelling. It makes possible all of the positives we seek from stories. Still, many hesitate, as if admitting problems and conflicts and their associated Risk and Danger is tantamount to admitting flaws and weaknesses.

Just the opposite. Showing audiences what you have had to overcome creates an image of greater strength.

Controlling your presentation of risks and dangers is a powerful tool in controlling audience engagement and emotional involvement in your story. If the story pops into your mind as being worth telling, then conflicts and problems along with the risk and danger they represent *are* there. They always are. You are the one who then gets to use them to enhance the effectiveness and power of your stories.

☐ ☐ *Back to the story we're trying to build.*

We started with "He went to the store." Unacceptably boring.

We added a goal and then an unsuccessful conflict. We need to change the conflict "He" faces to one that easily engenders element 6: substantial *risk and danger* for "him" to face in "He went to the store." A few paragraphs ago I said that physical risk and danger won't be nearly as powerful for most of your stories as emotional, social, and mental dangers. However, Hollywood movies often rely on physical dangers because it makes the storytelling easy. I'll use it here for the same reason.

> *He went to the store for some milk.*
> *A golden butterfly perched on the door handle, twitched its wings, and hissed, "You can't come in!"*
> **With a high-pitched whistle, the butterfly summoned his swarm of African killer bees, who blocked the front door and threatened his life.**
> *So he crept around to the back door and into the store to get his milk.*
>
> *The end.*

Better? Not yet. Now it feels like a cheap shot. You are likely muttering, "What's the point?!" and, "Why'd you bother to mention the killer bees if you don't use them in a story?"

We need another element.

■ ■ ■

ELEMENT 7: STRUGGLES

If I am going to include killer bees (the Bad Guys) in this story, you expect—no, your NSN demands—that our main character confront that obstacle en route to resolving his goal.

What you need is for "He" to *struggle*.

> **Struggle:** To contend, to engage, to exert a great effort, to fight, to stand against, to oppose

Readers will never appreciate success without first seeing and vicariously experiencing the struggle to overcome great problems and conflicts, face great risk and danger, to reach an important goal. That's the essence of powerful, influential, and effective stories.

A Telling Example

Baby duck woke up. "Quack, quack. Where is my mother? I need to find my mother."

There we have a cute, endearing character (babies are always cute), a goal, and plenty of danger. A baby animal in the wild will die very quickly without its mother.

Baby duck turned around. "Oh, there you are. Hi, mom."

See how totally wrong that seems? You need that duck to struggle to find his mother if you are going to pay with your time and attention to visualize this story.

Let's change it.

Baby duck woke up. "Quack, quack. Where is my mother? I need to find my mother."

Baby duck searched around the pond. No mother. "Oh, no! I need to find my mother."

Baby duck waddled to the cow barn. "Quack, quack. Is my mother here?"

"No," moo-ed the cow. "Your mother isn't here."

"Oh, no" sobbed the baby duck. "I need to find my mother." Baby duck raced to the pigpen. "Quack, quack. Is my mother here?"

"Oink, oink," said the pig. "Your mother's not here."

"Oh, No! Wailed the duck. "I need to find my mother."

Every time the baby duck fails to find its mother, *risk* increases—the likelihood of ultimate failure. Danger stays the same: if it fails, it will die. As risk increases so does story excitement and tension. It works exactly like a mathematical equation.

Go to the library and scan through picture books for young children. An amazingly large number use the exact story approach I outline above. It is always a winner. It will be a winner for you, too. Establish character and goal, problems and conflicts, risk and danger. Then don't make it easy for your characters. The more they struggle and suffer, the more empathetic and supportive your audience becomes.

Any kind of struggle will do.

Internally:	Over a decision
	Between competing goals
	Over self versus others
	Over uncertainty, a lack of information
	Over facing (or not facing) tasks, fears, etc.
Externally:	With enemies
	With the public
	With governments (authority figures)
	With boss and co-workers
	With storms, jungles, droughts, or army ants
	Against injustice, poverty, illness, etc. etc.

Don't feel that having to struggle is a sign of weakness. Struggle is a strength. It is a virtue. More importantly, it is a critical story asset and element if your audiences' NSN is to understand and make sense of this story as you intend for them to do.

☐ ☐ *Back to the story we're trying to build.*

We started with "He went to the store." Unacceptably boring.

We added a goal, conflict, risk, and danger. But we need for him to do something to deal with that conflict. We need to add element 7: *struggle* to overcome the obstacles we have created en route to resolving his goal. Here's a struggle:

> *He went to the store for some milk.*
> *A golden butterfly perched on the door handle, twitched its wings, and hissed, "You can't come in!"*
> *With a high-pitched whistle, the butterfly summoned his swarm of African killer bees, who blocked the front door and threatened his life.*
> **He risked his life, swatting and slapping his way straight through the attacking bees**
> *and into the store to get his milk.*
>
> *The end.*

Notice how much more satisfying the story is with the addition of struggle? No, it certainly isn't fully satisfying yet. But it is suddenly much *more* satisfying.

You will also notice that we are still missing half of the eight essential elements. Let's pick up the missing pieces.

■ ■ ■

ELEMENT 4: MOTIVE

Aren't you beginning to wonder why "He" would risk his life for a quart of milk? Couldn't he munch his chocolate cake for once without swilling a mug of chilled milk? Couldn't he pour OJ on his breakfast flakes just this once and skip the milk? Was that milk really worth risking his life?

You are now hunting for one of the most powerful and most overlooked of all of the Eight Essential Elements—element 4: *MOTIVE*.

Motive: The information that makes a goal important to a character

Motives are the answer to the question, "Why do they need to reach that goal?"

Motives give a character compelling reasons to struggle to reach a goal. While it is important to make *goals* tangible (and thus easy for audiences to visualize), no such restriction applies to motives. Motives commonly relate to the human condition: loyalty, faith, belief, peace on earth, fairness, justice, self-sacrifice, family, right versus wrong, greed, selfishness, lust, avarice, laziness, and so on and so on. It is usually true that any goal is backed by a complex web of interlocking motives.

Motives become critically important to you for two reasons.

1. Neural Story Nets need to know motive.

Motive is one of the first things each person's NSN invents if the source material (the story) doesn't provide it. In recent studies, test audiences 1) are almost always "wrong" when they infer motive (i.e., the motive they infer does not match the motive the writer intended) and 2) they consistently created more sinister, negative motives when left on their own than were intended or envisioned by the story creators. How often have you found yourself skeptically wondering, "Why did she say *that*?" and "What is he *really* after?" and "What is he *hiding*?" during a conversation with a co-worker, neighbor, or acquaintance? That is your NSN seeking a motive in order to make sense out of the incoming information.

2. Motive is a key element for empathy and identification.

Motive controls a story receiver's interpretation of both character and story. During my work on the DARPA research program I previously mentioned, I found that I could induce an audience to either identify with a story character or to reject her and treat her as the story antagonist by shifting only a few bits of character motive information.

That is an amazing statement to be able to make. In the next chapter, I will unravel the mechanisms of story influence. That process requires story receivers to identify with some story character. You can control and direct that identification process by matching the stated motives of your characters to the known group motives of your target audience!

Effective stories are not a hit-or-miss, cross-your-fingers-and-hope-they-get-it process. These specific Eight Essential Elements control reader and listener reaction to your story-based material. Motive is one of the most powerful and yet is one all too commonly overlooked.
Let me demonstrate how motive dictates how you relate to a character.

Once there was a shark, named Sharky, who wanted a puppy.

There is a character and a goal. Here are four possible motives that lie behind that goal and explain why Sharky wants the puppy. As you read each, pause and assess how the different motives affect your perception of Sharky and your attitude toward the story in general.

- *He was tired of doing chores. Let the puppy clean up the reef and make dinner.*
- *He was tired of eating tuna, tuna, tuna. A nice hotdog on a stick, perhaps.*
- *He was lonely and needed a friend. He had already eaten all of his old friends.*
- *He wanted to show that land and sea animals could live in peace.*

Most people experience radically different reactions to these various motives. The point is, motive in large part controls how listeners relate to character and story. When it's **your** story, allocate a bit of time to deciding which motives you will present to explain the importance of your story goals. Your audience will thank you for it.

Motive, in conjunction with goal, also creates basic story suspense. Suspense (literally being suspended between a question the story has made us care about and the answer to that question) is an emotion—a feeling we routinely experience while reading or listening to a story. Suspense and excitement are the two main drivers of story tension. Tension is what forces readers to push on through to the end. Excitement is created by risk and danger (in conjunction with the problems and conflicts that generate them). Suspense comes chiefly from goal and motive.

Neuroscientist V. S. Ramachandran (2004, p. 1), says, "Most of our behavior is governed by a cauldron if motives of which we are barely conscious." But our NSNs certainly are forever on the hunt for motives that lie behind and explain the behavior of those around.

The greater the motive—the more that story motives shift a goal from a "want" to an "absolute critical need"—the greater the story suspense. Let's use Mary and her ice cream as an example.

Once there was a girl named Mary who wanted some ice cream.

There is a character and a goal. By asking, "Why did she want ice cream?" we arrive at her motives. Consider these two alternate motives:

1. *She liked ice cream.*

2. *The king said that for a bowl of butterscotch ice cream, he would release Mary's father and not send him to die in the slave mines of Blek. Without her father to earn a wage, Mary, her mother, and her twin baby brothers would all starve.*

Which story would you rather read? Same character; same goal. But radically different motives. When you use more powerful motives to turn a goal from a mere want into an absolute necessity, you instantly create audience interest, empathy, and support. Motives link directly with both the head and the heart of an audience.

☐ ☐ *Back to the story we're trying to build.*

We started with "He went to the store." Unacceptably boring.

We added a goal, conflict, risk and danger, and we have made him struggle. Now we wonder, "Why would he risk his life for a quart of milk?" We need to add element 4: *motive*. We'll talk more about using motives in Part IV on Story Influence. But for now here's a motive that explains why "He" wants to get some milk:

> *He went to the store for some milk*
> **that would keep his deathly ill son alive**
> **until the doctor arrived.**
> *A golden butterfly perched on the door handle, twitched its wings, and hissed, "You can't come in!"*
> *With a high-pitched whistle, the butterfly summoned his swarm of African killer bees, who blocked the front door and threatened his life.*
> *He risked his life, swatting and slapping his way straight through the attacking bees and into the store to get his milk.*
>
> *The end.*

Keeping your deathly ill son alive is a noble and powerful motive. Notice how it affects your view of, and your relationship with, "He"? The act of risking his life for a quart of milk suddenly shifts from meaningless, pointless self-indulgence to a noble and worthy act of self-sacrifice. Bam! Instantly you begin to identify with "He," to empathize with him, and to root for his success . . . Or at least you would if we hadn't skipped over elements 1 and 2.

■ ■ ■

ELEMENT 1: CHARACTERS

Stories are about characters. Always have been; always will be. Stories are about characters—not about plots. Stories are not about what happens but about the characters to whom that stuff happens. Audiences won't care about events and information until they care about the characters involved in those events. Once they care about the characters, almost anything can happen, and the audience stays hooked. Your story characters are number one on the list of elements and should be number one in your heart—and in your story planning.

The place to start your story planning is by deciding whom the story will be about.

We got away with delaying thoughts about story characters in the story we are building for two reasons:

1. "He" in our original sentence identifies a character (though tells us virtually nothing about him).
2. It's still such a short story that you are willing to read it even though you don't yet know anything that makes "he" interesting or memorable.

Those conditions, however, are unlikely to exist in the stories you develop and share. Best to start with the character and let your stories build from there.

HINT

> *Writers' wisdom: It is close to impossible to retrofit an interesting character onto an existing story line, yet it is easy to fit a variety of successful plot lines onto an existing character.*

When your message is about a concept or about information, it often seems difficult to identify an appropriate character to use. Let's start with the basics. What *is* a character? Here are five key characteristics that separate characters from things and objects:

An effective story character *must*:

- Be a **physical** entity
- Be an **individual**
- Possess a **will** (be able to think and form intent and self-interest)
- Be capable of **acting** in support of that will
- Be able to **communicate** (express self)

The first two items on that list are often the most troubling for organizations and companies. You can't use a concept or idea as a character. "Climate change" won't work as a character, even if that is what you really want to write or talk about. Neither will "ending poverty." If you make it more specific, it might work as a goal. It certainly works as a motive. But it's a story killer if you try to make it your character.

I recently worked with a university biology department on their in-class use of stories. One prof wanted to use mitosis as a character. Doesn't work. You need to find a physical entity to use as a character and let what happens to that character demonstrate the concept of mitosis. Once she took the time to explore possible characters (instead of the chem and biology equations and reactions she wanted to focus on), the story suddenly came alive, became clear, and was fun in her mind—as it hadn't been in the many months she had been struggling to make it work.

Main characters must also be individuals. It just doesn't work to use an organization, a company, or a city as a character. We all know that those congregations of characters do not speak with a single unified voice and mind. Thus, audiences can't identify with and relate to those conglomerates. Audiences are never deeply engaged. You need to search for an individual to use in the story who will act as the representative surrogate for the larger group your information focuses on and is about. In Part V on Process, I'll discuss character selection at some length.

An "Interesting" Character Question

For now we'll move to the second key character question. What makes a character *interesting*? If audiences find your characters to be of interest, they will pay attention to your story. If they don't, they won't. Being interested in a character is different from liking that character. Despicable villains are normally quite interesting.

Take "interesting" literally: **being of interest**. You want audiences to be interested enough in your main story characters to file them into active memory, remember them, and to want to find out what happens to them.

Finding ways to make story characters (real or fictitious) interesting to audiences is often the hardest part of crafting effective stories. One of the worst things that can happen to your story is to have readers get to a key moment on page eight as a character reenters the story and to have the readers say, "Who's *that*? I don't remember him." The moment is lost. Engagement is broken. The story has failed.

Pause and think for a moment. What kind of information makes a character interesting? Physical description? ("She has two arms, two legs, two eyes, and hair on her head.") Personality description? ("She is nice.")

The answer is that *any* descriptive information can make a character interesting (including having two arms or being nice) as long as it differentiates this character from those around him or her. What makes a character interesting is any information that makes that character different (unique). Such information allows the audience to mentally tag and hold that character for future reference.

If that same character information helps the intended audience members identify with that story character, all the better!

As you'll see below, there are some categories of character information that are of greater general interest to audiences. People are always fascinated, for example, in character flaws. Still, there is no need to rely on such star categories to make your characters of sufficient interest that they can hold the audience's attention and interest. Anything that makes one character stand apart from the crowd will hold interest.

Bottom line: *If you want listeners to pay attention to **your message**, create a **relevant** and **interesting character** for them to identify with.*

■ ■ ■

── ELEMENT 2: CHARACTER TRAITS ──

Character traits are really just details about characters. Traits are information you share about your characters that is independent of their actions and involvement in the story. If a character lies during a story, that is an action. How she feels about having lied would be a character trait. If she lies most of the time, that's a character trait. Character traits reveal the character hidden under the skin.

The longer the story, the greater the amount of character information you'll need to create/find and share in order to keep your audience interested in your characters. For a short, one-minute story used during a talk or as an example on a brochure or blog, a character's name, job, and situation is often sufficient. At the other end of the spectrum, I know of authors who recommend that a 75-point background essay be written for every major character in a novel.

Here are what I find to be the most consistently useful categories of information to scan through to search for a couple of interesting tidbits that will make your characters interesting: their history (back story), physical characteristics, jobs and hobbies, hopes and dreams, talents and abilities, likes and dislikes, passions, voice, fears, and habits and quirks.

Any information that is unique, unexpected, or unusual in these categories will do nicely. The unique traits you use do not have to relate to the major events or struggles of your story. If they do play into the flow of the story, count that as a bonus.

This interesting information is revealed to the audience through the character's action and involvement in the story. However, they are character attributes that are independent of the story.

Once this mix of unique and interesting traits hooks audiences on a character, they tend to stay hooked—even if nothing happens in the story. Look at classic TV soap operas. You can go away for months. When you come back, the same phone conversation that was happening when you left is still in progress. We don't care. We deeply know and are mesmerized by the characters. We know their flaws, secrets, schemes, ambitions, agendas, and hidden motives. We know about their feelings of spite and revenge as well as their secret loves. And that makes us love them. It is the character traits that make us care about these story characters.

In Part IV on Story Influence, we'll explore how to use character traits to make your audiences identify with your story characters. During recent lab experiments, character trait and motive information showed the highest correlation with individual audience members' decisions to identity with, or to not identify with, a character.

☐ ☐ *Back to the story we're trying to build.*

We started with "He went to the store." Unacceptably boring.

We added a goal, conflict, and risk and danger; we made him struggle; and we gave him a strong motive to justify his struggles. At last we have come to the place where we should have started: to "him," the character. We need to identify who this main character of our story is (element 1), and we need to add element 2: the *character traits* that will make him an identifiable individual who is of interest to our intended audience. See how these additions affect your attitude toward this character.

> **Bob, a kindly bald man—bald ever since his severe reaction to a wasp sting when he was ten—lurched to the store on his skateboard (using his crutches to propel him down the street since one leg and one arm were in casts after his coke-bottle-bottom thick glasses fell off halfway up his last cliff climb, leaving him virtually blind to tumble 80 feet into a pine tree),**
> *for some milk*
> *that would keep his deathly ill son alive until the doctor arrived.*
> *A golden butterfly perched on the door handle, twitched its wings, and hissed, "You can't come in!"*
> *With a high-pitched whistle, the butterfly summoned his swarm of African killer bees, who blocked the front door and threatened his life.*
> *He risked his life, swatting and slapping his way straight through the attacking bees and into the store to get his milk.*
>
> *The end.*

Certainly, this particular story is now so extreme it slips into comedy and farce. But the function and effect of each of these elements is real, consistent, and potentially serve as powerful controllers of how your audiences respond. These same elements exist for any story you want to share. Your job is to dig them out and make sure that your audience's Neural Story Nets get the version of each element you want them to have and pass them along to the conscious mind and memory.

Seven of the Eight Essential Elements are now accounted for in that paragraph. Notice how automatically and naturally they blend together? Take out any one of these seven elements, and the structure crumbles. It stops making sense.

However, the story is still not engaging. You may chuckle at it. But you aren't drawn in to viscerally and virtually experience the story as you read it. Why? We're still missing one element.

The story still doesn't seem "real." You can't "see" it in your mind. You can't picture (or hear) the vicious bees (or the store or the street); you can't feel the wind drummed up by their pounding wings; you can't smell the dust swirling in front of the store; you can't hear the sound of the store door swinging open and shut or the muffled voices from inside. Why? One final element is still missing.

■ ■ ■

ELEMENT 8: DETAILS

Story details create pictures in audience minds. Every image you have ever "seen" in your mind and memory when you heard or read a story came from the details. We create stories, but we write details: character details, sensory details, scenic details, and event (action) details.

Audience members use the details you provide as a substitute for their own direct sensory observations—what they would see, hear, smell, taste, and touch if they physically experienced the story. Those pictures create a sense of reality in your mind. They make (allow) you to believe in the story as if you had personally experienced it. Studies have shown that you activate the same parts of your mind when recalling a story that you do when recalling a similar real-life experience.

One of the most quoted (and most overused) of all story maxims is "Show, don't tell." What does it mean? Give us the sensory, character, and event details that we would record on our own if we were there, and we will build a vivid and powerful movie of events in our minds. It's always the details that turn a lecture (telling) into a mind movie (showing).

An analogy: Picture yourself sitting in a Broadway theater just before opening curtain. House lights shut off. Even the green exit lights are dimmed. It's pitch black. On stage, you hear the actors shuffle out to their opening positions. You hear the curtain open. But you still can't see a thing.

Then one narrow-beam spotlight clicks on and shines down onto a chair on the right front corner of the stage. You know that you (and every other person in the theater) will turn and look at that empty chair. Even if someone speaks from the dark on the stage's left side, you'll still look where that spotlight points. If that light clicks off and another goes on to shine on the left side of the stage, you'll turn and look over there. Play directors use lights to control and direct your attention around the stage. And it works wonderfully well.

In a story, details perform the same function as those theater lights. Details control what the audience sees and what they *don't* see. When you include rich story details at one story moment, it is just like turning on a stage spotlight. The audience pictures that moment in the story. Leave out the details, and it is exactly like leaving off the lights in a theater. The audience overlooks that part of the stage or that moment in the story.

Just as theater audiences see only what is shown in the spotlights, story audiences see and retain only what you describe for them in rich detail. Details are your story spotlights. What you hit with details (a light) people see and picture in their minds. No light (no details), no mental pictures and no attention.

In this way, details allow you to control your audiences' minds. How? By allowing you to control the images (the pictures) they focus on, vividly visualize, and file into memory.

First design your story. Then ask yourself what pictures you want people to remember and stuff in those sensory details at the appropriate spots. If there are moments and aspects of your story you do not want an audience to focus on, pull back on the detail you use to describe that moment or that aspect.

What do story details look like? They "look" like what your senses would record if you were there. Consider the story we have been slowly patching together.

Here are two sentences from an early version without even the sparse details that I earlier included:

> *He went to the store for some milk. But a butterfly perched on the door handle and hissed, "You can't come in!"*

Now consider the same sentences with details as you might write them in a story.

> *His shadow seemed to shimmer in the rising waves of heat. Even dust swirls prancing down the rutted main street of town seemed to suffer from the heat. It seemed to punish the very land. He pulled off his wide-brimmed hat and wiped the sweat from his forehead with one sleeve. What a killer day for a trip to the store! With a glance of loathing at the relentless sun, he jammed his hat back low across his eyes and stepped onto the wooden sidewalk. The sound of muffled voices from inside the store slid around the double-hinged front door. The jingle of horse harnesses from two buggies faded as they rolled toward the south end of town.*
>
> *He reached for the store door latch and froze. Perched right there on the latch was a golden butterfly that seemed to glow with shimmering color like reflections from the brightest plate of polished gold. Almost too golden, too bright to be real. Actually holding his breath in wonder, he bent close to study the wondrous creature as its wings rhythmically twitched, antennae pawing at the air. With a defiant slap of its wings, the butterfly hissed, "You can't come in."*

Details are the fodder that allows us to create and visualize a scene in our minds and make it seem real. Viewed from another perspective, those same details also limit the pictures your mind is able to create.

If I say, "He walked down the sidewalk," you are able to conjure any image you like.

However, if I say, "He was an old, bent-over man so that, from the side, he resembled a human question mark. And he always wore a floppy, wide-brimmed hat on his walks—a hat so wide it almost drooped down to touch his shoulders; a hat that always hid his eyes in its black, impenetrable shadow. None of the kids had ever seen what color his eyes really were—or even if he actually had eyes!" you can't help but picture an old bent man with a floppy hat and hidden eyes. No one could hear this description and picture a young woman carrying a parasol. No one has ever stopped me from reading those sentences to say, "No! That's not what he looks like."

Details create pictures, but they also let you control (limit) the pictures your audience can visualize as they try to understand your material.

If details are that important to the success of your story, why are they the last item on the list of Eight Essential Elements? Easy. In the temporal sequence of story preparation, details are the last element to focus on. Use the other seven elements to create the story. Then as you write and edit it, focus on the details that will snap it into powerful and vivid life.

I once saw a TV interview of an elderly Florence, Italy, woodworker who made the most gorgeous doors I had ever seen. The interviewer asked him how he knew when the door was finished. He answered that it is never finished. He just keeps polishing and smoothing until they come and take the door away. The editing process of working on story details is much the same. You can always make them clearer, crisper, more specific, more unusual, stronger, and more powerful. You just keep combing over and over through the story trying to make each image more perfect in the mind of the reader.

One caution. Details don't come for free. There is a price to pay for spraying vibrant details throughout your story. Each detail slows the pace of the story a tiny bit. Each one sucks a tiny bit of energy (excitement) out of the story. You need to include the details. But you want to pay the smallest possible price for the story benefits they bring.

It is a form of cost-benefit analysis. You want to get the greatest image "bang" for every energy and pacing "buck" you have to pay. How? Work on each detail to wring the greatest possible imagery out of every word. Strive to make each detail more specific, unusual, unique, and vivid.

■ ■ ■

── THE EIGHT ESSENTIAL ELEMENTS ON PARADE ──

Those are the Eight Essential Elements. Those simple informational bits match the core informational mandates of the Neural Story Net as it struggles to fulfill its Make Sense Mandate. The NSN will obtain and use those specific informational pieces—either from you and your material or by its own invention, using its own Banks of Prior Knowledge.

In order to be engaged, the NSN is looking for an interesting character (character and traits) who has an important goal (goal and motive) but is blocked by some combination of problems and conflicts that create real risk and danger. So, the character must struggle to get past, over, around, under, or through these obstacles, facing the risk and danger, to reach the goal. These descriptions must provide sufficient detail so that the conscious mind will be able to form vivid and interesting images along the way.

Those are the Eight Essential Elements. Here they are in table form.

The Eight Essential Elements of the Story Structure

1. Characters:	The characters that populate essential character positions in the story.
2. Traits:	Selected elements of character description used to control receiver attitude toward, and relationship to, story characters.
3. Goal:	What a character needs/wants to do/get in a story.
4. Motives:	The sets of drivers that make a goal important to a character. Goals and motives are the primary source of story suspense.
5. Conflicts and problems:	The sets of obstacles that stand between a character and an established goal and block that character from reaching the goal.
6. Risk and danger:	The likelihood of failure (risk) and the consequences of failure (danger) created by problems and conflicts that a character must face. Risk and danger are the primary source of story excitement. Excitement and suspense are the primary sources of **story tension**.
7. Struggles:	The sequence of events a character undertakes (struggles) to reach a goal highlighted by the climax scene (confrontation with the last and greatest obstacle) and the resolution scene.
8. Details:	The character-, sensory-, scenic-, and event-specific descriptors used to create, direct, and control receivers' story imagery.

That is the essential framework, the architectural scaffolding, of every effective story. That frame still allows for infinite variety in the way and the order in which these elements are developed and revealed. It provides plenty of space for each writer and presenter to inject his or her own artistry and to emphasize his or her unique talents. But eventually, no matter how you construct and present it, your story must enter the mind of your intended audience and traverse the tightrope between sensory organs and conscious mind. That tight rope is owned and operated by the NSN. The Eight Essential Elements are your safety net to ensure your messages survive the crossing.

It is now possible to say what we really mean when we seek to create a powerful, influential, and effective story.

> *Effective story structure is: that character-based story organization that uses the Eight Essential Elements to provide the information required by the Neural Story Net in order to understand and to make sense.*

Remember, these Eight Essential Elements:

- Exactly match receiver neural information demands
- Explain how listeners hear and make sense
- Are the best guide to effective stories
- Control engagement
- Are the gateway to influence

And that makes them well worth your consideration as you plan, mold, craft, and edit your narrative material.

There is only one evaluative criteria, one metric, that really matters: Does you material (your messages, themes, and information) lodge accurately and vividly into the minds and memories of your intended audience so that they will readily recall them to affect their attitudes, beliefs, values, and behavior?

What I have presented so far are many of the most powerful and effective tools you can load into your personal story toolbox. Like all tools, the more you play with them, the more you use them, the better you will become at making those tools perform exactly as you want them to. As you gain comfortable familiarity with them, you'll soon find that you can intentionally manipulate these elements to change audience response in predictable ways. That is a very powerful, effective, and influential thing to be able to do.

I'll close this part of the book with a bare bones summary of the Eight Essential Elements. Use it as a shorthand checklist for the elements.

The **BARE BONES** Version of the Eight Essential Elements

_____ (Character)

Needed _____

Because _____

But _____

So, _____

Finally _____

Reading it from the top: _____ (an interesting character) needed _____ (a goal) because of _____ (motives). But _____ (problems and conflicts; risk and danger). So, _____ (struggles). Finally, _____ (climax and goal resolution).

That is just how simple, common sense, and basic the Eight Essential Elements are. All that is missing in this bare-bones version are the details with which you make the other seven come alive in your audiences' minds.

■ ■ ■

PART IV

IT WAS A DARK AND STORMY NIGHT ... HOW STORIES CREATE INFLUENCE

INFLUENCE IS THE NAME OF THE GAME

Now we can begin to put the Eight Essential Elements and story thinking to work. The "work" you need your stories to accomplish is to *influence* your intended audience: employees, volunteers, team members, funders, staff, students, those in positions of authority, and/or the public. You want to shift their attitudes, beliefs, values, knowledge base, and behavior. You want to inspire them, get their buy-in, persuade them, teach them, or enlighten them. You want to use stories to *influence*.

Actually, all stories try to influence. There is always a point: a seed, a message, or a concept upon which even the silliest of stories is anchored and that the writer wants the audience to absorb and consider.

You want stories that serve your particular purpose: not *stories* that get remembered, but stories that get *your messages* remembered. The key to understanding the process of creating influential stories is to understand the mechanisms through which stories so powerfully exert influence.

We have just finished laying out the Eight Essential Elements that create the structure of effective stories. Note, however, that none of those elements mentions the *receiver* of the story. They all describe the story itself, independent of who says it (or writes it) and of who hears it (or reads it). We started (in Part II) inside the brain and mind of the receiver, saw what the receiver requires, and backed from there to the essential structural elements laid out in Part III.

Still, even our Eight Essential Elements model evaluates a story exactly the same if it is presented to audience A as if it is presented to audience B. However, we intuitively know that different groups—different populations—respond quite differently to the same story.

While story structure is audience independent, story influence is definitely audience dependent. We must go back inside the brain and mind of the listener to see how story influence really works.

■ ■ ■

——— "I WAS WORKING IN THE LAB
LATE ONE NIGHT . . ." ———

Influence modeling must look at the audience and how they react to the story. This is where the recent DARPA-sponsored project Narrative Networks becomes critically valuable to our analysis. I was lucky enough to be a part of that study. The central thrust of that research effort has been to explore the neurological and cognitive mechanisms by which stories exert influence.

As part of my contribution to that effort, I was able to conduct a series of controlled lab experiments no storyteller has ever been able to conduct. My goal was to isolate the elements of story that most control test audiences' strong emotional reactions.

I say "strong emotional reaction" because in earlier testing, I found that stories that people described as "powerful," meaningful," "impactful," or "memorable" (all surrogates for "influential") were also ones for which they reported a strong emotional reaction, a tug, at and after the resolution point of the story. This "residual emotion" is the emotion that you carry away from the story that lingers after the story has been concluded. I find that this emotion is highly dependent on the nature of the story's **resolution** and thus, I call it **Residual Resolution Emotion (RRE)**. The experiments I describe bore out the central importance of this emotion in determining the potential of a story to influence an audience.

Without that lingering residual emotional component, people report being satisfied with a story. They report enjoying the story. They can find the story engaging, fun, or entertaining. But they *do not* describe it as impactful. Stories that listeners report as having "affected" them are also ones for which they report a strong level of residual emotion. The higher that emotional level, the bigger the reported affect.

From these experiments, I am able to conclude the following:

> *There exists a direct correlation between the strength of the ending emotional state of the audience and the magnitude of the influence that story can carry.*

That is a truly remarkable statement to be able to make. It gives you a specific, reliable tool to use to both understand and to control the influence your stories will have. By knowing your intended audience, you can design (or select) stories that will spark a residual emotion that correlates with the affect (influence) you want to achieve. Notice that I am not yet referring to the specific nature of the emotional reaction (though I will in a bit). I am referring now to the correlation between the magnitude of that residual emotion and the magnitude of the resulting influence.

Subsequent testing has confirmed this correlation and, as you shall see, has given us much more specific information about how it works.

For the experiment I mentioned, I chose one of my 10-minute stories that features two main characters (a father and a son in obvious conflict). My performance history with this story gave us a good baseline expectation for audience reactions and responses during our test runs.

In this story I watch a father and six-year-old son (Jeffery) stop at a small pond in an amusement park so that Jeffery can drive one of the remotely controlled plastic boats out in the pond. Jeffery seems totally unaware of the plastic boats and just wants to play imaginary games with the spoked wooden ship's wheel in his hands. His father demands that Jeffery watch the plastic boat and "play the game correctly!" Conflict ensues.

I reorganized the story to isolate each of the major story informational elements into separate story segments. (All character trait information for each character was crammed into its own section. So was motive information for each character, etc.) Admittedly, this produced an unusual flow for the story that I feared might detract from listeners' response as compared with that response I get from the baseline integrated version. However, I was greatly relieved to find that our initial test audiences responded much the same to this reorganized version as performance audiences had to the original.

I then created alternate versions for each of the major story sections by substantially altering the essential story element featured in that segment. (This gave me two different versions of the character descriptions for each major character; two different versions of the motives for each character; two different goals; etc.)

We video recorded me telling each possible version of each segment of the story. In this way, I could paste together the exact version of each segment of the story I wanted to use for each new test audience.

We recorded the stories in order to eliminate any effects minor variations in multiple live performances might have. Using the exact same video recorded segments for each audience meant that we would eliminate this performance variable and be able to directly trace differences in audience response back to the section-by-section selections I made in creating a story version for each individual audience to hear. I could change just one section between the versions shown to two different audiences, or I could change combinations of segments.

Doing this let me answer the question: What happens if I change this one part of the story? Or that one part? Or these three parts in combination? It allowed me to examine the effect of a story (element by element) in a controlled and replicable way. I would be able to literally watch which changes created strong shifts in reaction and which did not. I would be able to identify those elements/aspects of story that drive personal involvement and strong reaction and which do not.

You will recall that I described this experimental setup on the first page of this book. However, it is worth repeating that description here now so that I can put it in it context.

Each member of each test audience was wired to a 24-channel EEG system, was fitted with cardio and skin galvanic monitors, and had saliva swabs collected both before and after the story to measure oxytocin and dopamine levels. Video cameras recorded each person's reactions and movement throughout the story. After hearing the story, each subject filled out a written follow-on questionnaire about the story and its characters, and took part in a short oral interview.

I now held a great mass of data that linked specific story elements to real-time audience response and to their recorded brain activity. Those EEG charts let us search for known markers of engagement, empathy, character identity, transportation (being transported into the story), and—especially—emotional response. The questionnaire responses and interview discussions allowed me to quantify the audience perception of characters and story (and the shifts in those responses) and tie them back to the specific story shifts I had made for each individual audience.

No one had ever conducted this kind of detailed story assessment before. Did we find what we were looking for? You bet we did!

Here are the results we found that will be useful in your story work.

■ ■ ■

—— AND THE WINNING INFLUENCE ELEMENTS ARE ... ——

It turns out that while the Eight Essential Elements *are* essential to establish engagement, context, relevance, and meaning (necessary precursors to story influence), they are not all of equal importance in creating story *influence*.

Story influence hinges on several specific character positions in a story, on their goals and motives, and on the feeling the story's resolution leaves in you. We'll delve into each of these three. But first we need to see how they fit together.

We have all heard the term "story line." Most associate it with plot, with the sequence of events in a story. Forget that sense of the word. I want to lay out a much more significant and powerful (measured by the control it gives you over your stories) use of "Main Story Line." As used here, the Main Story Line is made up of the structural elements of story that were consistently significant parts of our test audiences' determination of meaning and impact (influence) of the story they saw.

Think of the Main Story Line as a straight horizontal line (see Figure IV.1 below) that runs from the story's main character (left side) to the resolution of that character's primary goal at story's end (right side). Along that left-to-right path, the line includes three characters (Main Character, Antagonist, and Climax Character), two key story events (climax and resolution), and two essential informational elements (the Main Character's goal and motives).

The Main Story Line

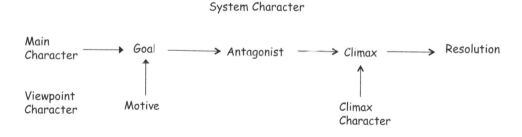

- **3 Characters**
- **2 Events**
- **2 Concepts**

Figure IV.1

Let's put those elements into sentence form. A Main Character (the character the story is centrally about) has a goal made important by a set of motives. However, the Antagonist blocks the Main Character from reaching that goal. Those two characters meet for the final time in the climax scene of the story. During that confrontation, some character (could be the Main Character, the Antagonist, or any other character in the story) acts to decisively determine the outcome of that climax moment. We now reach the resolution of the story where we discover whether or not the Main Character achieves his/her goal *and* how that character feels about this outcome.

Those are the elements that consistently and accurately predict and control the emotional response of audiences to our test stories. They are powerful cues for how you can control the reaction you get to your material and the influence that material is able to exert.

In reality, all of the Eight Essential Elements are accounted for here except for the details that will create the pictures that make the story seem real. We have a sufficiently interesting main character (character and traits), as well as a goal and motives for that character. We have the antagonist representing the problems and conflicts and risk and danger the main character must face. The main character's struggles lead to the climax scene. The resolution represents, of course, goal resolution: Did the main character get to that goal or not, and how does that character feel about it?

Notice, though, that there is an extra character position represented along the Main Story Line, the Climax Character. When I introduced the Eight Essential Elements, I defined element 1: Characters as "the characters that populate essential character positions in the story," not just as "characters." In order to understand story influence, we must talk about several of those key character positions.

■ ■ ■

STORY CHARACTER POSITIONS

Think of your stories as vibrant ecosystems. In every ecosystem, certain niches exist: top predators, herbivores, grasses, scavengers, decomposers, and so on. The specific species that occupy one of those niches in ecosystem A may well be different from the species that occupy that same niche in ecosystem B, but in every ecosystem *something* occupies each of those major niches.

Stories are the same. There are certain character positions that appear in virtually every story. We expect (actually it is our Neural Story Net that expects) to find some story character occupying each of these major character positions and performing the functions of that position. The way audiences relate to story characters is, in large part, controlled by the position (or positions) audience members perceive that the characters occupy, and this, in turn, seems to dominate how audiences relate to and respond to the story.

It's part of the Neural Story Net wiring and preprogramming. Every audience member expects to find some story character fulfilling these exact character positions. Actually, audiences *demand* that they do so if the story is to make any sense. We depend on these character positions to gain a quick understanding of the structure of the story. Someone, for example, must tell the story (the storyteller, or viewpoint character position). The story must be about someone (main character) who will always face some combination of problems and conflicts (antagonist), and so forth.

A character position is a story function that needs to be performed in order for the story to make sense. The actual characters in a story are the ones who must take on the functions of these character positions and fulfill the services required of those functions.

I found three character positions that consistently affected listener story and character evaluations and that seemed essential for effective and influential stories.

- **Main Character:** This is the character that the story is "about." It's "their story." Technically, the Main Character is that character whose primary goal is resolved at the resolution point of the story.

- **Antagonist:** The Antagonist is the physical embodiment of the greatest single obstacle blocking the Main Character from reaching his or her goal. In the climax scene, the Main Character will confront this antagonist for the final time in the story.

- **Climax Character:** At the climax moment of the story, *someone* will act to create the final outcome of that climax and define how the story will resolve. That character is often the Main Character, sometimes the Antagonist. But it doesn't have to be either of these two. In some stories a side character steps up to become the hero and "save the day," taking on the role of the western movie cavalry who always rode to the rescue (flags flapping and bugles blaring) just in the nick of time. They served as the Climax Character.

Whoever steps up to assume this Climax Character role and determine the outcome of the story climax (and face its associated risks and dangers) becomes a central figure in defining the meaning and impact of the story for the audience.

Many try to label this character the Hero. However, that title implies that the Climax Character always works toward, and always achieves, a positive outcome from the perspective of the Main Character and the audience. In many stories that is not the case (and it certainly isn't the most powerful and influential story structure).

Better to stay with the neutral title of Climax Character.

Test audiences needed two additional character positions to be performed. If these two positions are not represented, it creates confusion and reduced engagement. However, these do not, generally, affect audience reactions to and evaluation of the story.

You will notice that the System Authority Character and the Storyteller (Viewpoint Character) do not hold positions on the Main Story Line. They have to exist but don't necessarily affect story understanding, impact, and influence.

- **Authority Character:** Every story exists within some social structure or system (a school, a company, a club, an ecosystem, a family, a church, a kingdom, etc.), a system defined by lines of authority and by the rules that govern life within the system. Someone has to represent the authority of that system and wield that system's authority, responsibility, and power (teacher, king, manager, chief executive officer [CEO], governor, parent, priest, sheriff, emperor, chief, top predator, etc.)

- **Storyteller:** This is the character who tells the story, the character through whose eyes we (readers/listeners) see the story (often called the Viewpoint Character). The Viewpoint Character creates our perspective on the story. This character defines our attitudes toward the other characters. Changing storytellers changes not only the story that can be told but also how audiences understand and create meaning from the story.

    For many stories the teller is not a known story character; rather it is some omniscient observer (the narrator), someone who can be everywhere (without needing a Star Trek®

transporter), know everything (including the future), and sneak inside every character's mind to report what they are thinking and feeling.

Using an omniscient narrator makes the story writing and telling much easier but is not nearly as powerful as is using a story character as the teller of the tale.

Each of these major positions can, of course, have supporters, underlings, sympathizers, and minions in the story. There are often also neutral characters not associated with any of the story's central characters. Neutrals exist as background and as "local color" for the story but do not measurably affect the story's progress or outcome.

In a sense, these fixed character positions are like story shorthand, like story stereotypes that make it far easier to build an engaging mental picture of the story from the partial information that comes as the story begins.

As your Neural Story Net races through the process of making sense out of the initial pieces of a story, it searches for—and expects to find—some story character acting to fulfill these various positions in the story. Understanding which story characters fulfill these character positions is part of making sense out of the story. Certainly one character can fulfill several (even many) of these positions. The king (authority figure) could easily also be the story antagonist who, at the critical moment of the climax confrontation, has a change of heart and reverses himself to swing the climax in the direction of the main character (making the king also serve as the climax character). If the king is also the one who tells us the story, he adds narrator to the bevy of positions he fulfills.

Humans tend to be exceptionally good at correctly pigeonholing available story characters into these specific positions and at using their prior knowledge expectations of the nature and function of each position to flavor their impressions of each character.

If you would like to read more about the full range of character positions in different forms and genres of stories, I recommend the character role analysis done by Katherine Farmer in Utah. Published work on her research and model structure should begin to appear by early 2015.

■ ■ ■

GOT CHARACTER?

Here are the first findings that popped out from our test results once we were able to establish our experimental framework for assessing story influence. These findings lay out cues you can use to better craft the story messages and information you want to use.

1. **Changing motive and changing character traits dramatically changes listener reactions to those characters and to the story.**

   On a "likeability" scale of 1 to 10 ("likeability" is a questionnaire surrogate for "do you identify with this character?"), the father in our test story consistently rated between 1.8 and 2.4 (very low—audiences disliked him) when I characterized him and his motives as being a controlling bully. When I added a more sympathetic motive—but did not change any of his actions or speech—his likeability jumped to an average of 6.5! That's a huge shift created by the addition of two sentences in a 10-minute story.

   When I added character traits to Jeffery (the son) that made him seem mischievous and devious (again without changing anything that he said or did), it significantly lowered his audience rating. The same thing happened when I added character traits for Jeffery that made him appear to be arrogant and smug.

2. **Key character traits controlling that change relate to beliefs, personality, attitudes, values, motives, and interactions.**

   We experimented with a variety of the kind of character information we provided for our different test audiences. Some changes had little or no impact on our audiences. Some created instant seismic swings in audience attitude and perception. Of all the many types and categories of possible character information, those descriptors of a character that (when we changed them) consistently produced major shifts in audience attitude included beliefs, personality, attitudes, values, motives, and interactions. "Interactions" refers to the manner in which this character treats other characters during direct story interactions.

   With a few extreme exceptions, there were no absolute "good" or "bad" descriptions. The key question focused on whether I shifted the character description in a way that my target audience liked (that better matched the ideal values and beliefs of their perceived in-group) or shifted the character description away from that perception.

   This short list of character trait categories serves as an excellent guide for you to use as you plan and craft the characters you want your audiences to care about and to identify with.

3. **Motive Matching.**

   We found that the one piece of character information that most dramatically and consistently affected test audience perceptions of, and attitudes toward, each story character was the *motive* I gave to each of them. Certainly a tangible goal had to always exist. But it was motive—not goal—that affected audience attitude.

If the audience approved of a character's motives, if the audience felt that they held the same motives as a story character, they were strongly drawn to that character, approved of that character, and tended to adopt that character's viewpoint, attitudes, and outlook.

Let's call it *Motive Matching*. If you know what drives your target audience (their core motivations), then you can assign matching motives to the story character you most want them to care about and with whom you want them to identify.

In Part III, I showed the power of motive to influence audience attitude. Let me extend that idea here. Watch how your decision of whether a character's motives match your own values and attitudes dictates your identification with, or rejection of, that character.

A Telling Example	*Consider a Frenchman—we'll call him Jean Valjean—who wants to steal a loaf of bread. The question is why. If I say it is because the unfair and oppressive policies of the French king have so oppressed the common people that Jean is now unable to feed his family and, with the desperation of a father who cannot sit by and watch his daughter starve, he decides to turn to stealing, then I have Victor Hugo's opening to* Les Miserables, *a story that has inflamed and impassioned (and strongly influenced) audiences for over 100 years. Motive Matching. You identify with Jean's motives and so identify with the character.*
	If I said the reason Jean has decided to steal a loaf of bread is that he is addicted to the thrill of petty crime, you might be sympathetic, but you'd be unlikely to identify with Jean.
	What if I said that the reason Jean wants to steal that bread is because he can't stand the thought of letting others possess anything? This Jean is a wealthy nobleman who is obsessed with total control of his barony. What he cannot otherwise own and control, he is quite willing to steal. Now you are most likely to oppose Jean. Why? Motive inversion. His are likely to be in direct opposition to the values, morals, and beliefs that form the foundation of your motives and beliefs.

That's the power of motives to influence the allegiance of your audience.

Same character. Same goal. But change motive and you radically change how story audiences evaluate the characters and how they want/expect the story to end. That is, audiences' attitude toward the character (based on their evaluation of that character's motives) determines whether they want the character to achieve his or her goal or not and how each audience member will feel about the story's resolution when the character either does, or doesn't, achieve that goal.

Change character motive and you change an audience's emotional reaction to the story in predictable and controllable ways.

4. **It is always easier to change the audience's evaluation of the antagonist than it is to change their feelings for the main character.**

I mentioned that a small shift in character information for the antagonist (motive, in the example provided) created a large and dramatic shift in an audiences' evaluation of that character. However, the same statement cannot be made about changes to the main character (also the audience's identity character in this story). When I added a devious and sinister motive to Jeffery in our laboratory test story (he ignored the boats because he knowingly and gleefully wanted to torment his father), it only dropped his likeability rating from an average of 8.8 (strong identification) to 7.5—still a favorable rating.

It is almost as if once we latch onto a character to root for and to care about in a story, we turn a blind eye to any imperfections we later discover. We *want* them to be our hero! The point, however, is that it is much easier for you to shift audience response to your story by adjusting the characteristics and motives of the antagonist than to make changes in how you present the main character.

This observation from our experimental results exactly matches what I have observed on stage when I tell stories and what other tellers have reported to me. It is much easier to control story tension (remember: *tension*—the sum of excitement and suspense—controls *attention*) by shifting your description of the antagonist (the "bad guy") than by shifting your description of the main character (the protagonist, the "good guy").

■ ■ ■

THE IDENTITY CHARACTER
RULES INFLUENCE

All structural models of story revolve around identifying the story's *main character* and the *antagonist* (the physical embodiment of the greatest obstacle blocking that main character from reaching his or her primary goal). No, the antagonist does not have to be a person—or even a sentient being. It could be a storm or a mountain—as long as it is treated in the story as having a conscious will and consciously opposing and trying to block the main character.

Those two specific elements (main character and antagonist) tell you a lot about the organization and purpose of the story. It turns out, however, that they don't always tell you a lot about the story's potential influence.

I found that **story influence is dependent on the <u>identity</u> character.**

No, the role of identity character does not show up in anybody's structural model of story. No, there is no position for this character on the Main Story Line. What, then, do I mean by "identity" character?

Identity Character: **That story character with whom an audience member most closely identifies as they listen to or read a story**

When you find yourself thinking, "He (or she) is just like *me*"; "*I* do that, too"; "I think that, too"; or "That's *my* same situation!" you are identifying with that character. You suddenly hold something in common that is significant to you; you feel a common bond.

Suddenly that story character is part of your tribe, your in group, your profession, your type. You feel that you and the character hold values, beliefs, attitudes, goals, and driving motives in common. As soon as you make those associations, researchers tell us that you begin to identity with that story character, you care about him or her. You are interested in what happens to him or her. Your focus shifts away from the main character and the Main Story Line to a new *Influence Story Line* that puts your identity character into the role of main character.

That's all well and good if your identity character is, in fact, the main character of the story. Then the story is still about the character you care most about. The climax relates to your character. The resolution is about the goals of your character.

Problems arise, however, if your identity character is not one of those story characters who appear on the Main Story Line. Then the story is no longer about the character you care about. It is no longer relevant to you. Your engagement drops. The story's ability to influence you falls away.

These problems escalate if you identity with a story's antagonist. Your emotional reaction then tends to be the exact opposite of what was intended by the story's writer.

The identity character, of course, must be one of the available story characters. Still, I found that I could shift a few key bits of character information and predictably shift the audience's identity character!

Remember that the climax of the story (*main* character confronts *antagonist* for the final time in the story) and the resolution (resolution of *main* character's primary goal) are fixed. They won't change. And they are both about the *main character.*

However, audiences really care about the story of their identity character. If that character is not the story's main character, the significance and the meaning of those crucial story events will change dramatically depending on which character a particular audience member most closely associates with as their identity character. That same audience member will look at the climax and at the resolution from the vantage point of "What do these events mean for my identity character?" That answer could vary drastically, depending on who their identity character is.

What does a shift in identity character look like?

A Telling Example	*Imagine a coven of witches reading a version of Hansel and Gretel that includes an additional opening section in which the witch, persecuted by townsfolk, sadly moves out alone into the woods and builds a candy house to show that she welcomes children and visitors. Now the children arrive and begin to eat (destroy) the witch's house! Who will this set of readers identify with? How will they react to the children tricking and killing their identity character?*

A Telling Example	*Imagine learning that a young, kind-hearted wolf struggles to pass the final exam of Wolf School and please his parents and that to pass that test, he must successfully hunt and catch dinner for the wolf pack. You identify with him. You sympathize with him and then learn that the first place he goes on that hunt is a straw house where a pig lives. You have always identified with the industrious pigs fending off the evil of the Big Bad Wolf. Now the tables are turned and, even though the sequence of events of the story doesn't change, your reaction to them changes drastically.*

I was supposed to read Moby-Dick *in eighth grade. The school copies of the book had small print size, densely packed text, and many hundreds of pages. I was instantly put off and never read it. When I decided to actually read this classic in my twenties, I just happened to pick it up right after I had finished another book—one I loved—called* The Year of the Whale *(Scheffer 1969), an account of the first year. in a sperm whale's life. I deeply felt each of the whale's struggles and dangers. I rooted for them. I sweated for them. I shared in their triumphs—and in their losses. I swam the oceans beside them, saw the world through their eyes, and deeply identified with them. It was a great read, and I still recommend it to high school students thinking of careers in oceanography.*

Then I picked up Moby-Dick. *I instantly identified with the whale. That put **all** humans in the book into the role of hated enemy characters. The whale's final triumph was bittersweet. Hooray, Moby-Dick lived and escaped! Too bad he had to be hurt along the way. To me, that book screamed out that all humans are evil destroyers and trespassers and that whales are the noble best that our planet can produce. That is not the story interpretation an English teacher is looking for as she grades her class's book reports. When an audience member shifts allegiance to a different identity character than the one the story creator intended, it doesn't change the story, but it does radically change what the story means.*

One final example. My shortest story ("Brian and the Worms") is one I often use during workshops—because it *is* so short and because it is an excellent example of identity character.

One day after an all-night hard rain, little Brian got up and headed off to school. Just as the rain ended, as the clouds began to split apart and as beams of golden sunlight poured down through those growing holes in the clouds, splashing puddles of light across the sidewalk around him, little Brian walked to school.

That afternoon, on the way home from school, Brian found his mother waiting for him on the front porch, her fists jammed into her hips, her foot angrily tapping on the wooden boards of the porch, her eyes glaring down the front porch stairs at her son.

"Brian, what on earth happened to you today?! The principal called!"

"I know, Mom. I was standing right beside her in the office when she did."

Mother's finger jabbed at the air toward her son as she scowled. "She said you were an hour and a half late for school. You left on time.

Why were you so late?!"

"Welllll, Mom. After all that rain, all the worms crawled out onto the sidewalk. I was afraid that the sun would dry them out and kill 'em or that the mean kids would step on them and squish 'em. I had to put the worms back into the grass where they'd be safe . . . There were a lot of worms, Mom . . ."

And Brian's mother said, "Brian, I love you!"

Children and nonparents always identify with Brian. Mother is the Authority Character and Antagonist. This is the classic bully position (picture Darth Vader and the Evil Emperor) that we love to hate. Brian's goal is to get out of being in trouble. The madder I make his mother, the greater the risk and danger he faces and the more exciting the story becomes.

Notice that the crucial line in the story is Mother's final "I love you." With that line, she abdicates her role as antagonist and emerges as a sympathetic Climax Character. She determines how the final confrontation between Main Character and Antagonist will resolve itself.

However, to parents who identity with the mother, this story points to a path to salvation, to being the hero, to avoiding the trap of being the despised Antagonist. That thought never occurs to those who closely identity with Brian.

Same story. Same characters and events. But changing identity characters creates significantly different residual resolution emotions and different take-away meanings.

That's the controlling power of the identity character.

■ ■ ■

A BIT OF EMPATHY
FOR EMPATHY

The effectiveness of your stories depends, in part, on empathy. You must assume that your audiences will empathize with one or more of your story characters. That empathy is the first step to identity. It is a critical component of identity. If you can't empathize with a story character, how can you viscerally identify with them? How can you put yourself in their place in the story, walk a mile in their shoes, feel their pain, and experience the story through their eyes?

By definition:

Empathy: *The ability to understand and share the feelings of another.*

If I am going to identify with you, I must be able to imagine some reasonably accurate sense of how you feel. If I am going to be transported into the story, I must be able to feel the story through the stated emotions of my identity character as well as see the story world through their eyes.

But we now reach a potential cautionary tale for you to consider. We are becoming less empathetic as a nation, as a people. Many studies have suggested this trend over the past 20 years. A recent University of Michigan Institute for Social Research study looked specifically at this issue. The researchers "found that college students today are 40% less empathetic than they were in 1979, with the steepest decline coming in the last ten years." That's an enormous and alarming shift (Konrath, 2011, p. 196).

This study, however, used self-reported descriptors (not controlled observation) as the basis for their calculations. It is one thing for today's college students to describe themselves as not being "soft-hearted," or as not having "tender, concerned feelings." It is another for them to actually behave that way in their everyday lives and interactions.

Still, this study—that is supported by a chorus of rumblings from other recent studies—should serve as a yellow-flag warning. It is difficult to conceive of strong story identification without empathy. No empathy, little or no residual emotion; little or no influence.

Is this a signal to throw up your hands and give up? Not at all. This is a reminder not to take your stories and their structure and crafting for granted. I find that even the most jaded teenage audiences become highly empathetic during well-crafted stories in which they are offered a suitable identity character. This is a reminder that you have control of the story tools to make characters empathetic—motives, traits, and struggles (especially "unfair struggles nobly borne"). It is a reminder that it is more important for you to take full advantage of these tools *now* than it might have been 30 or 40 years ago.

All humans still do possess *mirror neurons* (those amazing and uniquely human neurons that allow us to figure out someone else's **intentions** [goal and motives] and *feelings* [emotions]) (Ramachandran 2011, p. 128). We all still possess the neural wiring and programming to see the world through another person's perspective (psychologists call this Theory of Mind, a name that has never made sense to me).

What this cautionary tale suggests is that it may now be a bit harder to break through the thickening veneer of detached toughness to base emotional attachments than it was in the past. The empathetic and emotional reservoirs are still there. You and your story just need to drill a bit deeper to reach them. It is a call for careful crafting and design of your stories. It's not hard. It's not extra work. But it does require conscious consideration of the design you present.

■ ■ ■

THE STORY INFLUENCE LINE

It's time to revise our model of the Main Story Line to reflect the elements responsible for a story's ability to exert—even to amplify—influence.

The Main Story Line identifies that core elements of a story. It diagrams the flow, purpose, and structure of the story.

The Story Influence Line is based on the Identity Character (the character a specific audience most closely identifies with) not on the Main Character (the character that the story is structurally about). The story follows the events of the Main Character. The story's potential to influence an audience member, however, follows those same events through the eyes and perspective of the Identity Character.

This shift has huge implications for how you design and analyze your own stories. The Story Influence Line won't necessarily tell you where the story is going or how it ends. But it will tell you what the story means and what impact it will have.

In some stories, and for some audience members, the Identity Character may be only marginally involved in the story that is being told. Such audience members are unlikely to be emotionally and personally involved in the story's events.

An example will help put this dilemma in perspective.

A Telling Example	*Peter Pan (Main Character) has Hook as an Antagonist. But what if you identified with Wendy? Who opposes **her**? Not Hook. It is Tinkerbell that takes on the role of Wendy's foe. Why? Tink is jealous of the attention Peter pays to Wendy. Now look at the end of the story. Wendy loses. She doesn't get Peter. Tinkerbell wins. She does. Consider how that shift of identity character would alter your view of the story's plotting development and resolution.*

If a story is to be influential as well as engaging, the story—as seen through the eyes of the Identity Character—must be as compelling as it is when viewed through the perspective of the Main Character.

What does this mean? It means that the Identity Character must have a tangible goal within the story and must struggle toward it. It means that there must be some story character that acts to block the Identity Character from reaching this goal. We will call this character the Foe Character. The Foe Character must be a physical story character or an anthropomorphized element (animal, storm, river, mountain, ocean, snake, etc.) against whom the Identity Character struggles. Finally, it means that we must learn about the resolution of the Identity Character's goal before story's end.

Are these informational elements for the Identity Character *always* in a story? Certainly not. It depends on the character with whom you identify in the story. However, when these Identity Character elements are missing, the story will not be powerfully influential for those audience members who have linked with this particular story character.

The elements shown on the Main Story Line structurally define the story. To evaluate story influence, you must substitute the Identity Character and the Foe Character onto the diagram in place of the Main Character and the Antagonist. This creates the Story Influence Line. (See Figure IV.2.) Notice, also, that I have included Residual Resolution Emotion as part of the Story Influence Line. That is a measure of the emotion audiences are left with as the story ends at the resolution point. I'll discuss its importance for understanding and calculating story influence in another section or two.

The Story Influence Line

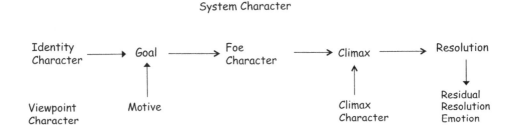

- 3 **Key Characters** + 2 **Supporting Characters**
- 2 **Events**
- 2 **Concepts**
- 1 **Lingering Emotion**

Figure IV.2

Now look at the climax scene and at the story's resolution point. These are both fixed structural elements in the story and haven't changed even though we have changed our perspective to now view the story through the eyes of your Identity Character. Are both story moments (climax and resolution) relevant to the Identity Character–Foe Character struggle? Does the story's resolution create meaning for the Identity Character?

In effect, you must view your story as two stories twisted into one. The story elements related to the Main Character's story will determine whether the story will make sense, be understandable, and be engaging.

Those story elements that relate to the Identity Character's story will determine whether the story is relevant, emotionally powerful, and influential.

It becomes extremely complex to determine how an audience member will emotionally respond to the story resolution if his or her identity character drifts away from the main character.

HINT

Story advice: Adjust and edit your stories (especially by controlling character motives) so that your target audience *will* identify with the main character of the story.

Your audience will care most about, and will follow, their identity character. If you don't know who that is, you lose control of the story, its meaning, and its messaging.

Here is what we learned from our lab experiments:

- **Stories lose power and influence when the identity character is separated from the main character. They also lose some power when the main character/identity character is not the viewpoint character (the one through whose eyes we are supposed to vicariously view and experience the story). For the most powerful and influential stories, tell it through the eyes of your target audience's identity character.**
- **Stories gain power and influence as the viewpoint, authority, identity, and foe characters assume positions along the story's Main Story Line.**

■ ■ ■

THE GOODNESS SCALE

I have mentioned in-groups and out-groups several times. These are important social research concepts that explain much of our behavior—from why we feel so strongly invested in the success of sports teams to why neighboring tribes and cultures are willing to slaughter and torture each other. The in-group is "us" and "we," and we are good. The out-group is "them" (really, almost any second- or third-person pronoun), and they are, by definition, bad. You can read more about the power of these pronouns in *The Secret Life of Pronouns* by James Pennebaker (2011).

In stories the Identity Character and the Foe Character represent these two mutually exclusive opposites. The questionnaire responses of our test audiences showed that the higher the regard with which they held the Identity Character, and the greater the depth of their disdain for the Foe Character, the greater the power, impact, and influence potential of the story. I was able to link those feelings to the specific language that our audience members used while describing their impressions of these two key influence characters.

As a first step in using this information, I created the Goodness Scale. This scale gives audience members a chance to place a character on the following scale based on their evaluation of the character's motives and interactions during the story.

	+10	Angelic
		Heroic
		Good
		Kind
		Right
The		Innocent
		Fair
Goodness		Desirable
	0	Neutral
Scale		Undesirable
		Unfair
		Guilty
		Wrong
		Bad
		Mean
		Cruel
		Evil
	−10	Demonic

While the vocabulary of this scale is fairly self-explanatory, we found that it also presented a good quantitative estimate of audience personal involvement and engagement in the story. It also provided a way to quantify the effect that changes in character description have on audience engagement and on their sense of story power. For example, if I sprinkle in a bit of new sympathetic wording in order to shift the audience's evaluation of the Foe Character from an 8 down to a 6, what does that do to their perception of the meaning and effect of the story?

The Goodness Scale is a linear scale. However, my story performance experience (confirmed by the experiences of many other longtime tellers) suggests that the *effect* is not linear. Especially as an audience member's evaluation of the antagonist approached maximum negative description, his or her residual emotional charge increased rapidly and dramatically. I knew that this nonlinear multiplier effect somehow depended on the residual resolution emotion felt by audience members.

■ ■ ■

THE POINT OF THE RESOLUTION

Kahneman (2011, p. 387) describes a series of experiments by psychologist Ed Diener. Test subjects were asked to evaluate an overall experience: a described fictional life (or a vacation) in which the end was emotionally different for the rest of the description. If, for example, a person was described as having lived a happy life—except for the last two years that were painful and unhappy—test subjects tended to describe that fictional person as having lived an *unhappy* life. The same was true of a described 10-day vacation that was described as happy except for the last 2 or 3 days that were unhappy. Test subjects, again, tended to describe the vacation as unhappy.

In story terms, Diener confirmed that the resolution emotion (the feeling you are left with at story's end) overshadows a story listener's evaluation of events *during* the story. Influence is dominated by the resolution and the residual emotion it evokes in story receivers. We call that final emotional state the Residual Resolution Emotion.

The resolution point of a story keeps rearing its head each time we discuss story influence potential. The resolution is a statement of how the story ends. The way a story ends is monumentally important to how audiences view the story and to determine what it means to them. I call it the *Resolution* because that is the story moment when the main character's goal is resolved. Either the character gets to his or her goal or he or she does not. We also at that same moment need to know how the main character feels about that resolution.

Goal defines story ending.

Once there was a girl named Mary who wanted some ice cream.

There are only two general options for the resolution point of this story: Either Mary gets her ice cream or she doesn't, and she must give up her hope of getting it.

If the main character has been successful in the confrontation at the climax, there are no more obstacles standing in her way. Her goal is there for the taking. There are two questions audiences need to have answered at the resolution:

- Does the main character actually achieve her primary goal?
- How does this character *feel* about it?

It is not automatic that a character will seize a stated goal once it is finally laid out before them.

A Telling Example	*Once, a boy named Edgar wanted to be elected class president. So he blackmailed and intimidated others in the class who also wanted to run. He hired thugs to scare off his competition on their way home from school. The students were terrified of Edgar and grudgingly, hatefully, voted him into office. At that moment he realized that being class president was going to be a lot of work! What he really wanted was a friend, not work. But he had thought everyone would want to be friends with the class president. Now that he realized that wasn't the case, would he still accept being president?*

And every reader wants to know: "So? Did he accept the job and become class president?" And they need to know how he felt at that moment.

This is where Joseph Campbell's classic hero's journey fits in. A character leaves on a quest with a stated goal, only to return and, because of personal growth along the way, realize that the original goal no longer has any meaning or appeal. He has grown past it. The hero *could* claim the original goal but chooses not to.

At a story's resolution point, audiences always need to know if the main character actually *does* accept the goal, and the audience needs to know how that character feels about it: overjoyed, saddened, relieved, bittersweet, resentful, hateful, and so on. Any of those emotions are possible at that moment of goal resolution. The ending emotional state of our Identity Character will guide our own residual resolution emotion.

My findings on the Residual Resolution Emotion are one of the most powerful and useful results of my lab experiments. We care deeply (and are deeply affected by) the emotional state we are left in at the end (resolution point) of a story. The degree to which we are affected (changed or influenced) by a story is, to a large extent, determined by the emotional state the story leaves us in at its resolution.

That is an incredibly powerful and useful thing for me to be able to share with you. This residual resolution emotion is the other central piece of the influence puzzle.

I am reticent to use more acronyms than absolutely necessary and have resisted using the initials for Residual Resolution Emotions to this point. However, it is a big mouthful, and I am going to use it a lot in the following paragraphs. For a few paragraphs I will use the initials **RRE**. I hope you will forgive me.

Here is what I found:

1. **Either positive or negative RRE can be effective and influential.**

   Most stories created for entertainment purposes are designed to leave audiences feeling satisfied and entertained but complacent. Wrongs have been set right. The world is back in balance and order. We found that these emotionally neutral endings have little to no influence on audiences.

That is the problem with wrapping purposeful stories up in a neat and tidy bundle at the resolution. It provides no motive for the audience to act, to change behavior. (After all, the problem was solved quite nicely without the audience's help. So, there seems to be no need for them to be ready to jump in next time.)

Using stories that end with all returning to normal can make the audience feel good but will never entice them to change attitudes, beliefs, values, or behavior.

2. Strongly positive, and strongly negative, RRE are *both* influential, but they affect audiences differently.

The conventional wisdom cautions storytellers not to end stories with a downer, with a negative ending. Certainly if your goal is entertainment, that's true. If your goal is to leave listeners feeling good, it's also true. However, if your goal is to *influence* (create a change in beliefs, values, attitudes, and behavior), if you want listeners to *act*, to *do* something, then our lab experiments (linked to other ongoing research) suggest that it may not be the best advice.

Hear that? **You DO NOT have to resolve your story with a happy ending.** We found that happy endings do not motivate immediate action nearly as well as negative endings do!

For a while I thought that *all* positive RRE were ineffective, that they did not exert influence. I came to that initial conclusion because laboratory experiments typically measure influence (behavioral or attitude change) by comparing test subjects' willingness to donate to a cause before and after the story. Any change in their behavior (willingness to donate some of their own cash to a cause) is considered to be the result of story influence.

When I fed audiences story versions with strongly positive RRE, we noticed little or no change in donations immediately after the story. Finally I realized that strongly positive RRE work on a different (much longer) time scale than do strongly negative RRE.

Both can be effective. Both represent powerful story influence. However, my results suggest that they affect audiences in significantly different ways.

3. Strongly positive RRE serve as ideal in-group role modeling.

It turns out influences from even the most positive RRE don't translate into immediate behavior changes. In addition to our results from my fictional test story versions, I analyzed over 80 stories used in different parts of the Arab world as motivational stories. Almost three fourths of these stories featured positive resolutions. The main character achieved his or her goal (often martyrdom), was rewarded for it, and felt good about it.

Yet, none of those stories drove people out onto the streets to protest. None sparked riots. None inflamed angry mobs (as did many of the stories with strongly negative endings). So, why were these positive RRE stories so commonly and often used?

By "strongly positive" RRE stories, I mean stories that audiences describe as eye opening, gripping, influential, forceful, compelling, arousing, motivational, inspiring, impressive, "it got to me," commanding, powerful, heroic, life altering, or epiphinous.

When I analyzed the internal structure of these stories, I found my answer. Strong RRE stories that hold the potential to influence don't just feature positive outcomes. They feature critically important positive outcomes (goal and motive) that hung precariously in doubt (risk and danger and struggles) and that were finally successful specifically and primarily because the receiver's identity character did what he or she did. In other words, critically important success was achieved because the identity character acted. The take-away meaning for listeners is clear: "I should do that same thing, myself—when the appropriate situation arises." These stories define ideal future behavior.

We also found that when the story's outcome is *not* in serious jeopardy and doubt during the story (a function of piling sufficient conflict, problems, risk, and danger in the character's path to create real suspense and doubt), the story is not perceived as powerful and does not exert strong influence.

We found that positive story resolutions (evaluated from the viewpoint of the audience's identity character) might—might—influence some unspecified future behavior but do not drive immediate and near-term actions and behavioral shifts. Positive resolution stories *can* modify values, beliefs, and attitudes and *can* serve as role models for those unspecified future events (if a memory of the story is triggered during that event). But they do not tend to alter near-term behavior. It's as if the audience concludes, "I'll keep that story in mind for later."

A Telling Example

Lori Silverman describes the following example in her 2006 book, Wake Me before the Data Is Over. *Lands' End® created a corporate philosophy: Guaranteed. Period. The challenge was to get all employees both to understand and to adopt this attitude. According to Sandy Johns, Lands' End's learning and development manager, they finally settled on a system that worked: stories. Lands' End trainers shared stories about employees who had taken the authority to do whatever was necessary to make customers happy.*

According to Jackie Johnson Gaygill, "When new employees hear the story of Nora Halverson who sent her husband's cuff links off to a customer because the ordered ones were on back order, they understand the extra effort our people are expected to extend to serve our customers. They learn it more deeply than a lecture or mandate could ever achieve." (p. 137)

Lands' End has now compiled booklets containing stories that demonstrate how individual employees go the distance for customers. The stories have not only increased commitment to Lands' End philosophy, they have enhanced a sense of belonging, camaraderie, and team building among sales employees.

That is positive Residual Resolution Emotion at work.

4. Strongly negative RRE create a demand for action.

These are the stories that spark immediate action. The more negative (distressing, unacceptable, despicable, enraging, etc.) the story's resolution is for the audience's identity character, the greater the tendency for that audience member to take immediate action (donate, protest, write letters, boycott, riot, etc.). It is as if they feel compelled to correct the situation and bring the story to a satisfactory resolution. Emotionally negative story resolutions are incredibly powerful and effective as drivers of immediate (short-term) behavioral shifts.

Audiences describe these stories with descriptors like abhorrent, heinous, loathsome, despicable, detestable, outrageous, atrocious, intolerable, horrible, enraging, terrible, evil, hateful, cruel, unacceptable, infuriating, hurtful, malicious, vicious, criminal, mean, insulting, awful, shocking, horrible, repulsive, catastrophic, or just plain *wrong*!

Good examples abound. Two of my favorite examples are the fast-food training story and the September 30, 2000, Muhammad al Durrah incident in the Gaza Strip.

A Telling Example

The Counter Girl Training Story

A 19-year-old girl went to work at a fast-food franchise as her first job. After three days of training that emphasized customer service, she was assigned to a cash register at the counter. She was to take orders, make change, bag orders, and hand them to the customers. Midway through her shift that first day, a young man walked up to her position. He smiled. She smiled. He ordered. They chatted a bit. She gave him his change. She bagged his order and placed it on the counter. They chatted a bit more. He smiled again and left.

Only as he was stepping through the doors onto the sidewalk did she realize that he had left his bag of lunch on the counter. Remembering the training emphasis on excellent customer service, she grabbed his bag, vaulted over the counter, and ran after him.

She caught him on the sidewalk and gave him his bag. He thanked her profusely and gushed appreciatively. Feeling pleased and proud, she hustled back into the store . . . and was promptly fired for abandoning her post and her cash register.

That's a strongly negative RRE. It feels wrong, mean. You hear the story and want to object, to protest. Stories like that get used in training sessions because they are amazingly powerful drivers of participation and discussion. No one shrugs and sits back complacently after a story like that. The powerfully negative RRE make you need to do something to make it better.

Muhammad al Durrah. There are several versions of this film clip on YouTube.

A Telling Example

This surfaced in October 2000, supposedly as footage shot by a French news team during an Israeli excursion into the Gaza Strip. To the sound of sporadic small arms fire, the footage shows a man (Muhammad al Durrah) hustling his son of 11 or 12 behind a small section of cement wall for cover. The boy weeps in fear and huddles against the wall. The father alternates between ducking for safety himself, holding/protecting his son, and glaring up over the wall at the invaders who are off screen and somewhere across the square. You can palpably feel his fear, concern, and rage.

The camera cuts to the next shot of Muhammad sitting against the wall with a vacant, glassy-eyed stare as his son lies dead in his lap, dead from a bullet shot through his head.

It never mattered that the footage was later shown to be faked. The target audience (young Palestinian men) identified with Muhammed. When he proved impotent to perform the most basic of fatherly duties (safeguarding his son) because of the Israeli soldiers, the target audience was enraged. Riots sparked across much of the Arab world. It became the most effective recruiting and fund-raising piece for the most extremist factions of the Palestinian and Arab communities. Within weeks, however, it was forgotten by all save the researchers. Negative RRE spark immediate action but not necessarily long-term change.

Here is a more general form of the negative resolution story. Person A suffers from cancer, homelessness, mental illness, discrimination, crop failure, climate change induced flooding, and so on and so on. You tell the story of person A. It ends in failure. (Person A succumbs to cancer or loses her home, or dies on the street, or commits suicide to escape the bondage of forced prostitution by human traffickers, etc. etc.) The theme (as well as the closing line of your story) is: You (story receiver) can make sure this doesn't happen to person B (or animal B, or scenic wilderness B, etc., etc.).

You're placing the story receiver in the role of climax character, making him feel responsible for how the climax of the next person's story is resolved. ("If you had come along with the help and support we seek, person A could have survived.") That's the power of a negative Residual Resolution Emotion to induce immediate action.

Thus, we found that it is relatively easy to manipulate the resolution point of a story and thereby also affect either desired component of audience response—immediate behavioral response or long-term attitudinal and belief shift. Story users, then, need to decide what they want to achieve by telling a specific story to a specific audience and should adjust the story accordingly.

■ ■ ■

PUT THEM ALL TOGETHER AND THEY SPELL . . . MATH EQUATION!

Through all of our experimental interviews and our analysis of test audience questionnaire responses, we kept circling back to the same few indicators that seemed to predict how a particular person would respond to all of the other story elements.

I was finally able to boil it down to three key questions that led directly to the controlling variables described above. Data analysis also showed me that these three key questions consistently corresponded to the magnitude of story influence.

1. Who is this story really about for *me*?

This is an obvious one. This question identifies the identity character. It also includes, however, an evaluation of how strongly the receiver of the story identifies with this character. Earlier, I described that evaluative process as the Goodness Scale.

The identity character also serves as the prime representative of the audience's in-group in the story. The identity character is part of "us." The character traits and motives ascribed to this identity character serve as in-group defining characteristics and what are at risk depending on the story's resolution.

2. How bad is the ending for my character?

The story ends when the main character's primary goal is resolved. Audience members evaluate the emotional meaning of that resolution point by deciding what it means for their identity character. The identity of the Climax Character also strongly affects how audiences interpret and feel about a story's outcome. This internal calculation leads to determining the Residual Resolution Emotion (RRE). While my wording of this question implies negative outcomes, it can be either positive or negative.

3. Who can I blame for it?

Now we identify the foe character. As with the identity character, this answer must include a quantitative evaluation of how repugnant and loathsome this foe character is to that audience member.

This answer also identifies "them," the target out-group. If a story influences listeners to act, that action is usually directed against this out-group.

I found that I could combine these three variables into a simple equation that expressed the Influence Potential of a story. The equation has been called the Influence Potential Equation (IPE). (In Department of Defense circles, they prefer to use the word "Radicalization" and call it the RPE: Radicalization Potential Equation.)

The IPE, then, is expressed as:

$$IP = RRE \ (D_i - D_f)$$

Where   IP = Influence Potential (−60 to +60)

RRE = Residual Resolution Emotion evaluated from the viewpoint of the Target Audience (in-group); varies from −4 to +4

D_i = Characterization Score for the Target Audience's (in-group's) Identity Character (0 to +5)

D_f = Characterization Score for the Identity Character's Foe Character (out-group representative) (0 to −10)

Our research group and several other storytellers tested this equation with a variety of audiences and situations, and with a wide variety of story types, over a six-month period. I developed a reliable list of audience vocabulary words to associate with each possible numerical value for D_f, D_i, and RRE in that equation.

When I used audience responses to score the stories, I consistently found that stories with IP scores less than −45 or greater than 45 were consistently described with words that research has associated with influence (powerful, moving, memorable, touching, etc.). When I was able to test stories with scores in this range in the EEG lab, neural researchers consistently found the neural indicators of empathy, transportation (being deeply transported into the world of the story), strong active memory, and indicators of belief and acceptance. Those all suggest, and are linked to, influence!

I am not suggesting that you whip out your slide rule and do the math for your stories. I *am* suggesting, however, that you pay careful attention to those three key influence variables when you select, edit, evaluate, or develop the purposeful stories you want to use.

■ ■ ■

STORY WORK

We have now explored the tools and story elements that you can use to influence story engagement, power, effectiveness, influence, context, and relevance. The next part of this book lays out a step-by-step process for systematically applying these tools and techniques to your story work.

This section on story influence is a lot to swallow on one reading—especially when piled on top of the concepts presented in Part II and the Eight Essential Elements of effective story structure developed in Part III.

A quick summary review of the elements and process of creating story influence is appropriate before we dive into the details of the process.

1. **Engagement.** Use the Eight Essential Elements to guide you toward creating engaging stories, ones that will hold your intended audience's attention.
2. **Context and relevance.** Consider your intended audiences' Banks of Prior Knowledge and their core concerns and motivations. Will this story make sense to them? Will it be instantly recognized as being relevant?
3. **Identity character.** Knowing your intended audience, anticipate who their identity character will be. Adjust the story as needed to make this character the story's main character and to control how your audience will view and evaluate this character.
4. **Foe character.** Identify the probable foe character for your audience's identity character. Consider how that character is described and what drivers (goals and motives) exist in the story for that character. Adjust the story information and wording as needed to control how negatively your audience will view this character.
5. **The story influence line.** Try to bring Viewpoint, Authority, Identity and Foe characters onto the Main Story Line. (That is, design the story so that the Main Story Line and the Influence Story Line merge into a single line.) Can you combine characters so as to give multiple character roles to a single character? The more you are able to condense the story onto the characters and concepts presented in the Main Story line, the greater the resulting story power.
6. **Resolution point.** Decide how you will end your story. Design that ending point to create the Residual Resolution Emotion you want to create in your intended audience—remembering that the magnitude and the nature of the RRE will control the nature of the influence your story exerts.
7. **Identity and Foe descriptors.** The IP equation tells us that the potential of your story to exert influence is proportional to the distance on the Goodness Scale between these two key characters. They must seem real and believable within the context of your story. They must fit with their function within the story. However, the more you can add traits and motives that drive these two characters toward the extremes on that scale, the more powerful, effective, and influential your story will be.

8. Details. Work on story details that will bring key scenes and moments to vivid and compelling life.

One important aspect of your use of stories to serve your purpose is still missing. We have talked about the story. But we have not yet talked about forming the message (the take-away, the information, the pitch) you want the story to carry straight to the conscious mind and memory of your audience. That final piece comes into play as we walk through the process of building effective, purposeful stories in Part V.

■ ■ ■

PART V

SEVEN STORY STEPS:
STEP BY STEP

This is not a "writing" book. I have not included guides for actually writing, crafting, and editing your opening hook, building a climax scene, controlling character dialogue, managing story tension, and so on. There are plenty of worthy detailed writing guides already in existence.

However, what good is a good story that doesn't accurately and powerfully deliver your messages through your audiences' Neural Story Nets (NSNs) and into their conscious minds? You don't want audiences to simply remember your stories. You want them to vividly recall your information, messages, and images each time they remember one of your stories.

These seven Story Steps are designed to weave your information and messages into the core fabric of your stories so that it will be difficult for your audiences to remember one without also vividly recalling the other.

Stories uniquely *engage*. No engagement, no attention. Ergo, no influence. However, the elements of effective story structure do far more for you than just engage and hold attention (though, goodness knows, that is a mighty and monumental task in itself). Stories:

- Create context and relevance
- Match the information demands of the Neural Story Net (NSN)
- Ensure minimal NSN distortion
- Increase emotional involvement, empathy, and identification
- Drive memory and recall
- Improve understanding of story information and concepts
- Create power and influence potential
- Drive the Make Sense Mandate: the process of making sense and meaning
- Make it vivid and visual (show, don't tell)

Am I saying that everything should be organized, planned, and presented in story form? No. I am not. If you want the power and benefits of story, you must provide the core elements of effective story structure. (See Part III.) That can, at times, be a daunting task. There are times when space and time limitations preclude your use of stories. Effective story development does take time (both in the development and in the delivery) and space.

What I *am* saying is this: It is always worth *considering* the use of effective story thinking and story structure. If you can't, if story structures just won't work for the information you want to share, or for the points you need to make, then you need to remember that each audience member's NSN *will* still use story elements and story structure to fulfill its Make Sense Mandate. Be forewarned and plan accordingly. This is where *story thinking* becomes more valuable than the final stories themselves.

Let's look at the seven-step process of creating purposeful stories. They are:

1. Define the target **audience**.
2. Create your **theme** and "take-away" message.
3. Search for a core **metaphor** and image.
4. Create **relevance** and **context**.
5. Adjust for "real-world" constraints.
6. Define/develop story **characters**.
7. Build the story **elements**.

Notice that the place to start is not with the story. The story comes last. Developing your core information and tailoring it for your intended audience is where you need to start.

One note before we start, and it is, I think, one of the most central of story development concepts.

HINT

> ### Create First, Write Second
>
> Don't worry about writing your stories down right away as you develop them in your mind. In fact, writing is counterproductive for your developmental purposes. Research has shown that each time we *say* something or describe something, we automatically create new sensory detail for that thing we describe. Having created that new detail, you can no longer distinguish between the *new* detail and the *original* detail. You file it all back into memory as original detail.
>
> The positive side of this detail-creating process is that each time you *talk* about a new story, you create more detail for it—so there will be more vivid details available in your mind when you finally reach the point of committing yourself to specific language on this story. And the same thing happens when you doodle or draw the story, or when you act it out.

HINT

> Say your story into a smartphone. Tell it—simply talk about it—while you record. Then listen and mentally edit. Record it again. You'll find it is both a time-efficient and an extremely effective way to develop your story material before you commit to specific written language.

■ ■ ■

STEP 1: WHO'S LISTENING?

What's This Step For?

The first thing to establish is what drives your intended audience so that you'll know if your messages and information will resonate with them. In story terms, your goal is to lay the foundation for creating context and relevance.

What You Need to Remember

I have mentioned several times that successful stories are audience specific, that you should write from the audience's Banks of Prior Knowledge, and that you must consider what *their* Neural Story Net will do with your information and your story.

Every effective story is target audience specific. The story happens in *their* mind, based on *their* Banks of Prior Knowledge.

You need to know as much as you can about the audience you want to reach. Certainly you have more than one principal audience. For now pick an audience type (associates, managers, students, public, customers, regulators, clients, etc.) that currently requires your attention. For this exercise, focus exclusively on that one audience.

What to Do

Make three quick lists about this one target audience.

List A: Characterize

Characterize this audience. Can you specify their age, background, education level, interests, geographic region? Can you characterize their prior knowledge? What do they know and believe about your topic? How aware are they of you, your organization, and your topic? Can you identify their cultural assumptions, norms, values, expectations, history, myths, and so on?

This list need not be extensive. It's a quick what do you know about them and what do they know about you list and will prove extremely useful in Story Steps 3, 4, 6, and 7.

List B: Issues and Problems

List what you perceive as the top problems, concerns, issues, gripes, and complaints for this specific audience. If your themes and stories don't relate to these, they won't be relevant.

That list represents the negative side of your intended audience. Pick the top two. We'll come back to these items in step 2.

List C: Motives and Beliefs

Flip to the positive side for the final audience list. Make a list of what motivates them, what resonates with them, what gets them excited, and what they deeply believe in.

Keep each answer in the form of a simple declarative sentence. Again, mark what you think are the top two or three.

HINT

Look for audience "hot button" issues that relate to your information or general theme.

Make sure your stories and take-away messages clearly link to these issues. It will make it much easier for you to create relevance, to engage, and to hold their attention.

What It Means

These three lists provide ready-made entry points to your target audience, approaches that will readily engage them and hold their attention. You'll use these lists so that your audience will readily perceive context and relevance from your story material. We'll get back to these lists in the future steps.

■ ■ ■

———— STEP 2: SAY SOMETHING! ————

What's This Step For?

In this step you'll define exactly what core messages you plan to communicate with each story and what you expect those story messages to accomplish.

This is the question at the very heart of your communication. What do you want to say? What do you want your audience to know, to remember, and to carry away from your communication? Assume for the moment that your stories have successfully engaged your audience. Now you have their attention. What are you going to do with it? What is it that you went to all this bother to deliver into their minds and memories?

What You Need to Remember

In story terms, we are looking for your *theme*.

> **Theme**:   *The central point or concept; the unifying idea*

A common substitute term for theme is "**take-away message**." Your theme is what you need for your audience to accurately remember; what they must carry away from your communication; your point and purpose; the thing you need for them to vividly see and accept.

Stories are extremely efficient at vividly delivering a theme to an audience —*a* theme— singular. Multiple themes tend become muddled when shuffled together in a single story, their impact seriously degraded.

What is it about you, your organization, your information, your concepts that you need your audiences to get and to remember?

It is important to get these thematic statements in a form that easily translates into story structure. Write them as simple declarative sentences. Try to avoid compound and complex sentences.

Think of these theme statements this way: Someone—let's call him Bob—reads your material or listens to your presentation. As Bob first walks away, a friend stops him and asks, "What was *that* all about?" What do you want the first sentence that comes out of Bob's mouth to be in response to that question? That sentence should match your theme if your material successfully delivered a clear and concise theme statement to your audience.

Certainly you will have different core messages for different audiences (employees and associates versus funders, versus volunteers, versus clients, versus the public, versus customers, etc.). More accurately, you will have different expressions of, and aspects of, your core messages that you will want to communicate to different groups and to different audiences. Each of these messages should be grounded in your core beliefs, values, and attitudes and extend from a practical expression of those core values.

What to Do

In this step you will create two short lists.

List A: Your Theme

Write down the core messages or information concepts you want to communicate to the audience you used for step 1.

Were your sentences vague and general, or did you create resonant, powerful statements that will be easy to build into resounding stories? Avoid qualifiers, limitations, and caveats. Be bold! This is what you want each audiences to remember and believe.

"Give me liberty or give me death!" "I regret that I have but one life to give for my country." Those are thematic statements. So is "We turn gun barrels into plow shares." So is Lands' End core theme of "Guaranteed. Period."

Adjust your sentences if need be.

List B: Your Desired Outcome

There's one more list to create. Another short list. What is your *desired outcome*? Surely you must have something specific you want to accomplish with your story-based material, something you want to *happen*.

How do you want your audience's attitudes, beliefs, values, knowledge and *behavior* to change, to be different *after* your information than it was *before*? What do you want them to do? To say? To think after they have absorbed your material? How does that thinking represent a change from their previous thinking?

Be as specific as you can. Write down in simple, single-sentence form your desired outcomes.

Look at your sentences and answer these questions. Is each statement:

- A clear statement of what you want **THEM** to **do** or **think?**
- An *action statement.*
- An *action IMPERATIVE!* (What they will feel that they *NEED* to do?)
- **Emotionally** (viscerally) loaded!
- An inspiring, alluring, and *demanding* **vision** you want to plant in their minds?

I realize that that is a lot to ask of a few simple declarative sentences. But take a few minutes to hunt for words that make your desired outcomes seem both essential and also soaringly resonant. English now contains well over 1.1 million words. Most have multiple meanings and uses. The words you want to use are there, if you'll dedicate a few moments to finding them.

HINT

Make sure that the climax character of your stories either represents your theme or employs your theme to achieve a positive climax outcome. If the outcome of the climax scene is designed to be negative (likely when the Residual Resolution Emotion [RRE] you want to create is highly negative), then it should be clear that the absence of your theme (your concept, information, or organization) is what turned that outcome away from main character success.

What It Means

You have now written two lists about you: what you want to communicate and what you want to happen because of that communication. Let's consider these in conjunction with lists B and C about your target audience. The central question is (it's really just a restatement of the central seller's question I included in the Economic Event section of Part II):

> *Will stories based on these themes be likely to create these results (outcomes) with and for this audience?*

Let's break it down into three sequential gateway questions that will be easier to answer as you examine your four lists.

1. Does the outcome you defined clearly solve the top audience problems (sources of pain) that you listed?
2. Will the themes you list clearly make this audience see how *you* can lead them to that outcome?
3. Will your themes and information engage the audience drivers and motives you listed (create context and relevance)?

If your answer to all three questions is "Yes!" Great! Wonderful! Magnificent! Proceed to the next step. You are on course to develop an effective, powerful, and influential story that will admirably serve your purpose and needs.

■ ■ ■

STEP 3: PICTURE, PLEASE!

What's This Step For?

Create a single powerful image in both words and visual imagery that represents the central theme identified in step 2 for this story.

We humans don't remember text very well. We do, however, vividly remember pictures and the emotions that go with them. Thinking visually now makes effective story crafting (step 7) much easier.

What You Need to Remember

You are far better off thinking *pictures* than thinking printed words as you plan, develop, shape, and edit your stories. Think pictures and specific story moments—like freeze frames from the movie version of your story.

Treat story planning like movie storyboarding. Define the pictures (combined with other sensory images) that dominate the various moments and scenes in your story.

By far the most important of these images is the one (or ones) that your audience will associate with your theme. Design this image *now,* and later you'll be able to successfully wrap a story around this image, and it will help carry your theme or core information. You will use story details to repeatedly paint this image into your audience's mind and to link it to your theme statements.

When you think of verbal pictures, you are into the realm of **metaphor.**

> Metaphor: Ascribe tangible, specific, and vivid characteristics of some **known** concept onto an **unknown** or unknowable concept in order to better understand the latter

Metaphors start with something your intended audience knows well (something that exists in their Banks of Common Knowledge) and attaches selected attributes of that thing or concept to this new thing or idea that they don't know well. Metaphors let us think we know the unknown by attaching the same kind of concrete attributes and traits to it that we hold for the things we know well. Finally, metaphors also typically carry an emotional edge that instantly engages and holds attention. In so doing, metaphors create powerful dominant images. They take over people's visioning as well as the ensuing conversations and discussions.

For our purposes, treat metaphors and similes both as metaphors. Metaphors and similes light up exactly the same brain regions and create the same kind of images in human memory.

Metaphors are tailor-made for describing your story characters (something definitely unknown and unknowable to your audience until you provide the metaphor; "John was Abe Lincoln honest") and new—especially complex—concepts you want to introduce ("A black hole is a giant vacuum cleaner that sucks in everything around it: dust, dirt, rock, even light!").

A Telling Example

A few years back I was consulting with a navy research group assigned to figure out how the navy would use and relate to cyberspace 30 years into the future. But first they had to define and describe what they meant by cyberspace. The group members had debated and argued over the definition for weeks. I said that they needed a good metaphor to unite their thinking. They nodded, looked at me, and said, "Do it!"

I wracked my brain that night and came up with what I thought would make me their instant hero: "Cyberspace is like a new ocean for the navy to explore and dominate." I laid it on thick, even saying computers were like the ships that sail this new ocean. I likened exploring cyberspace to a Roman galleon entering a new sea, mapping the boundaries, searching for dangerous rocks and currents.

For the first time in the three days I had been there, all 30 members of the research group agreed on something. They all agreed that they hated my metaphor. The one thing they had agreed on was that they didn't want to make cyberspace look like a three-dimensional physical space. I was crushed.

Yet—and this is my point about the power of even rejected metaphors— every time I overheard a conversation in the hall or in someone's office for the next day and a half, they always began with, and referred back to, that metaphor. They hated it and rejected it. Still, its imagery was powerful enough to dominate their thinking and talk. That's how powerful metaphors are.

There is only one way to judge a metaphor: either it creates an image that supports your message and position or it doesn't. If it does, use it. If it doesn't, treat it as you would a dreaded and deadly virus that must be locked into a deep, dark vault and never allowed to see the light of day.

If you'd like to read more on the interaction of human brains, human language, and metaphors, I recommend work by Lakoff and Johnson and have included two of their books in the references.

What to Do

Some find it is easiest to start with the picture and then back into a metaphor-like wording to express it. Others do better starting with the metaphor and then developing a visual image that represents the metaphor. You are best served by doing what comes more easily for you.

What idea represents everything you love about your theme? What would physically represent that theme to you? What traits do you want to transfer from you audience's know domains to the new domain (you, your organization, your information, etc.)? What emotions do you want to attach to that image? What physical images (animals, musical instruments, vehicles, plants, trees, parts of nature, etc.) come to your mind when you think of your theme? What qualities of your theme get you excited? What well-known physical thing is already associated with these traits and qualities?

Take a few minutes and play with traits, words, and images that might build into an effective metaphor for you. (Note: I find that metaphors are one of those things that come to you primarily when you think you are thinking—or dreaming—about something else.) Don't panic if nothing powerful emerges in the first two minutes of your search.

Draw it. Sketch it. Doodle it. Describe it out loud and add detail to the picture as you do. Actually put your image on paper.

HINT

Remember to think about what elements of the image will create the emotion you want people to feel when they recall this image. Add notes and detail to the picture to help you remember the emotion you want to create around this image in your audience's mind. Your story will develop this image and that emotion and wrap both around your theme.

What It Means

Great—even adequate—metaphors do not 1) fall from trees or 2) hang from the bottom branches with the easy-picking low-hanging fruit. Often they never come. But they are always worth a bit of struggle to locate and to craft. That effort—even if it doesn't literally produce a working metaphor for your themes and for your story—always seems to sharpen the story and the imagery story listeners develop in their minds. Even if the storyteller/-writer doesn't notice this visual improvement.

Metaphors are physical, visceral, and highly visual. They typically suggest vivid, emotion-laden images (remember, engagement is emotion-laden attention) that can serve as your theme picture.

It's time to advance to the actual image that will represent and symbolize your theme in the mind of your audience. If you were able to create a useful metaphor, that should translate directly into a picture image.

HINT

Is this picture a visual representation of your theme (step 2, list A)? If someone sees (or remember) the image, will the theme automatically pop back up with it? If not, change the picture. Also check to make sure all aspects and elements of this picture are accessible to the Banks of Prior Knowledge—the experience—of your audience (step 1, list A).

■ ■ ■

STEP 4: ON TARGET?

What's This Step For?

This is a check to ensure that you will be able to establish the critical elements of context and relevance for your story material. Your target audience will not pay attention to, or remember, your information if they do not perceive its relevance and context.

What You Need to Remember

Context and relevance are essential prerequisites for active memory. Minus those two perceptions, your audience members are highly unlikely to pay the attention to your material that you desire.

What to Do

For the theme, outcome, and metaphor you have created, answer these questions as a final audience relevance check:

- Why should they **"buy"** this information and **"pay"** with their time, thought, memory, and attention?
- What will make them first stop and be engaged?
- How will they use what you want to share? Will they see value in that use?
- How will your information fit in with what they already know and believe?
- Why will they see that they need it?
- What will make them accept your story and information?
- How will it benefit them?
- How will you make them see that benefit?
- Do you see how they will answer the question, "What does this have to do with *me*?"

The last question in this list is the most important. You should be able to easily answer this for your target audience.

HINT

What It Means

If you can answer these questions, you should be able to successfully engage your target audience. Your step 1, list A information should be consistent with the answers you identify here.

■ ■ ■

──── STEP 5: WATER COOLER WOES ────

What's This Step For?

In this step you will assess the effect of your "real-world" limitations on the effectiveness of your story.

What You Need to Remember

Reality has a way of raining on virtually every parade, of popping every rising story balloon. Of what reality do I speak? The reality of the constraints and limits that you face every day. Every program, office, and individual works within a complex web of real-world constraints. (Limits on budget, time, and space. Constraints by policy, dictate, established audience mandates and expectations, previous programming, etc.)

No one works in a vacuum, and no one is allowed to focus on story development to the exclusion of everything else. More likely, the demands of "everything else" force you to wedge in scattered moments for story work.

This step is a quick check to make sure that the normal real-world constraints and limits of your work environment won't prevent you from delivering to your target audience what their Neural Story Nets require in order to be engaged and to make sense of your material.

Your intent here is to compare your vision of the "ideal for this story" to what you will actually be able to deliver and to then be sure that the story will still serve your purpose.

What to Do

This step consists of a seemingly simple two-part question. As you answer, focus on part 2.

Part 1: What limits do the reality of your situation place on your stories and on your development of them?

Part 2 (the more important part): How will you still make sure that this is an effective story? Your audience won't care about your limitations and constraints. They will judge only the resulting story!

The heart of overcoming office constraints is to build up—over time—a stock of powerful, flexible, engaging stories that you can quickly mold to your immediate purpose and to link with the themes and take-away messages you want to deliver to any specific audience.

Create a *Story Culture* in your organization

Create an organizational **story culture**. Make it known and believed from the top to the lowest levels (and, yes, this is a good mission for a set of stories) that:

- Everyone is responsible for building the organizational story.
- Everyone has stories about their work, their experiences, their learning, their observations that are important.
- The organization values, wants, and needs these individual stories.

Then provide:

- Time and venues to share stories horizontally within groups
- Mechanisms, person power, and time to collect these stories and to catalogue and archive them
- Training on story structure, crafting, and telling to story coaches spread throughout the organization who are mandated to spread a growing awareness of the sources, form, nature, and value of individual and group stories and of the elements of effective story.

What you will quickly find is a treasure trove of valuable real-life stories that are worth their weight in "gold-pressed latinum" (as they say on *Star Trek: Deep Space 9*®).

What It Means

Your target audience will not consider the constraints that affect you. They will consider and judge only the story material you provide. Your job is to identify and circumnavigate (or otherwise overcome) those limitations so that you can deliver to your target audience what their Neural Story Net requires.

After you establish an organizational story culture, you will soon find that the stories you need for every occasion already exist. In the vast majority of organizations, companies, agencies, departments, and schools, these stories have simply never been sought out and collected.

■ ■ ■

STEP 6: CHARACTER CENTRAL

What's This Step For?

In this step you will begin to actually define and shape the story that will carry your information and images. This means that—finally—you will begin to plan the Eight Essential Elements you developed in Part III. The process begins by defining the main character and other core character positions that will inhabit your story (elements 1 and 2). In step 7 you'll cover the remaining six essential elements.

What You Need to Remember

The purpose and core content of this story is already defined. But not the story itself. All effective stories are about characters that occupy key character positions (not plot, not information). Effective stories are character based. Theme and metaphor give you the seed—the purpose—that launches a story. Once that's in place, the story begins when you identify the main character and then other key character positions.

HINT

> A successful story character must:
>
> - Be a physical entity
> - Be an individual (not a group or organization)
> - Possess a will (be able to think and form intent and self-interest)
> - Be capable of acting in support of that will
> - Be able to communicate (express self)

The main character must:

1. Be the story's main character

The main character must have a goal and motives. That character must face real problems and conflicts and face the risk and danger created by them. This character must struggle to reach that stated goal. At the story's climax moment, this character must confront the final obstacle (normally the antagonist), blocking him or her from that goal. At the story's end, we will find out if the main character got the goal of if he or she failed to achieve it.

That is the minimum required of a story's main character.

2. Allow you to present and explain your information and messaging

You must be able to easily present your information and thematic messaging by telling the story of this character. Your information has to flow naturally and seamlessly as you tell the story of this main character.

3. Be the target audience's identity character

Adjust character traits and character motives as needed to help the target audience identify with the main character. Build empathy for the main character by increasing risk and danger, main character struggles ("unjust burdens heroically borne"), and the nobility (in the eyes of the target audience) of the main character's goal.

4. Be an easy story character to develop

Can you easily develop a complete story around this character (real or fictional)? How much effort will be required to research or collect the information you need for story development? How hard will it be to mold that information into an effective story?

If your fledgling nominee for main character has passed these checkpoints, congratulations! You have a grand and coveted main character to use in your story.

HINT

The keys to **successful story characters**:

1. Make them *relevant* to, and of *interest* to, your audience.
2. Give them goals and motives *relevant* to, and *important* to, your audience—as well as critically important to the character.
3. Use motive matching to ensure identity.
4. They must face *real risk and danger*, and they must *struggle*!
5. How they resolve their goal determines audience resolution residual emotion.

Does this main character of yours have to be a real person? Not at all. I see three general options.

1. **Real human characters.** Here you tell the stories of actual people.

   (+s): Instant relevance and context with that person's identity group; authenticity. These are the actual, factual stories of real people that your target audience can relate to.

   (−s): You are limited to what actually happened and what was actually said. You can't fake it and improvise. You can't add parts to the story that didn't actually happen—even if they are important to making your key points.

2. **Fictional characters.** Here you use obviously fictional characters to tell your story.

   (+s): Fictional characters (think cartoon or stick-figure characters) do exactly what you want them to do, present the exact concepts you want to present, and convey your theme perfectly. You can draw them, their traits and motives, and their situation to exactly match those of your target audience in order to gain buy-in and target audience identification with your main character.

(–s): You need a strong opening hook to the story because many will initially view a cartoonish story as not important or relevant to them.

3. **Prototypical characters.** These are seemingly real people, but they are actually nonexistent. "Joe the Plumber" is an example of a prototypical character used by the Republican Party during the 2012 presidential campaign.

(+s): If the character creates strong identity for the target audience, this character can create a powerful and compelling story.

(–s): Dangers abound. If people suspect that your prototypical character is, in fact, fictional, and if you have not already claimed that he or she is pure fiction, then *YOU* lose credibility with this audience. There is also a risk that they will focus on "Who is *that*?" and not on the information revealed by what the character does.

What to Do

I find that the most efficient approach to picking a main character is to build a quick matrix of possible characters (on one axis) and the information you'll need to have about each character (on the other axis). As you fill in the boxes with "yes," "no," or "maybe" to indicate if that particular bit of information is readily available for that potential main character, you will quickly identify the one for whom you have the most essential information and that will make your story development the easiest and most successful.

Here is a sample matrix to show you what I mean. You may not want or need to consider all of the categories of information on the vertical axis for any specific story. Remember, this is just a tool to make your job easier, not a course mandate you are required to complete and turn in.

■ ■ ■

THE MAIN CHARACTER CHECKLIST GRID

Type of Information	Character 1	Character 2	Character 3	Character 4	. . . . . .
Theme*					
Information*					
Metaphor/Image					
Outcome*					
Identity*					
Traits					
Goal					
Motive					
Enemy					
Risk and danger					
Struggles					
Clear climax					
Resolution					
RRE*					
Hook					

Needed Grid definitions:

*Theme:** Can you easily emphasize your point and purpose by using this character as a main character?

*Information:** Will you be able to fit in your information using this character as the story's main character?

*RRE:** Residual Resolution Emotion

*Outcome:** Will this story lead to the Resolution and RRE you want to create?

*Identity:** Will your target audience be able to identify with this character?

Other Key Characters to Identify or Create

1. Antagonist/Foe:

What force or obstacles oppose your main character? Can you make these seem bigger (add risk and danger)?

2. Climax Character:

Ensure that this Climax Character either represents, or employs, the thematic messages and core information you wish to convey through each purposeful story. The take-away message should be that your concepts, approaches, and information made the difference or (if you choose a negative resolution and RRE) that your information would have made the difference.

3. Viewpoint Character:

This is the character that tells the story. I recommend that this be either you (the narrator) or the Main Character. Many other options are possible. But I advise you to keep it simple and straightforward.

4. System Authority Figure:

Unless the Authority Figure also serves in one of the three roles that appear on the Story Influence Line, I recommend that this not be a fully developed character. All that is required is that your audience understands the system of authority (rules, laws, and enforcement) within which the story takes place. In most short (several-minute) stories a generic title for this character will suffice (king, principal, parent, bank president, CEO, etc.)

What It Means

Characters are the lifeblood of your story and your primary tool to elicit engagement and attention. If you have identified or developed a workable main character and those other few key supporting character positions, then the story will engage and hold attention. If you have crafted your description and development of these characters so that their motives, goals, actions, and interactions will develop and project your theme and take-away messages, then CONGRATULATIONS! You are in possession of an engaging, effective, and influential story.

■ ■ ■

STEP 7: WRITE NOW!

What's This Step For?

This, finally, is the step in which you actually write, edit, and craft your story.

What You Need to Remember

A quick recap of where you are. You have done everything except develop the actual story (or to shape, edit, and focus an existing story—if you have one readily available). You have struggled to define the theme and its related imagery. You have forced your potential main characters into the glare of the runway spotlights.

Now it's time to put this story together and use it!

Remember, though, this is still a story. It is easy at this point to get carried away with and by your story—even after all of your prep work and planning. Remember to regularly check to make sure that the story still delivers your point and your information.

Many books and other guides already exist for the actual process of story writing. I have written several, myself. In *this* book I wanted to walk you through the process of effectively merging your information into the fabric of an emerging story (or to edit your information into an existing one). Rather than launch into a writing guide, I will restrict myself to offering a few key tips, reminders, and suggestions for where and how to spice your programs, documents, and presentations with jolts of effective and influential stories.

With the decisions from the first six steps well in hand, you are in position to build an effective and powerful story. Now that you know it will serve your purposes, you still need to make sure that it will serve the story needs of your audience.

What to Do

Here is a short story checklist to help you remember the story elements and concepts we have developed in this book. Remember:

- To use the Eight Essential Elements to engage and hold the attention of the audience
- To develop and manage story tension by controlling how you present the risk and danger your main character faces.
- To build that tension toward a climax moment.
- To resolve the primary goal of the main character—and make sure that that resolution creates the Residual Resolution Emotion you want to create.
- To make sure that the outcome of the climax is controlled by the use of (or concept of) your take-away theme.
- To manage the core Influence Elements.
- To develop an adequate hook (question) at the opening. (It need not be worthy of a modern thriller novel. A one-sentence question that introduces your topic will certainly suffice.)

- To use your theme (take-away statement) and desired outcome as a litmus test, as a measuring rod, to regularly check the developing story to make sure it still serves your purpose.
- To focus on details and on struggles. More struggles and more sensory details are always beneficial.
- Finally, to edit, edit, edit. No one ever got it right the first time (or even the second).

HINT

Keep your main story image (step 3) and thematic take-away message (step 2, list A) right in front of you as you write the story so that you'll be sure to weave the story around them.

Don't worry about the pictures you want to place firmly in you audience's minds until after you have settled on the final flow and order of the story. Then go back and pile in the details at those key spots to create those important images.

What It Means

By the time you reach this final step, you must trust that you have woven your messaging, your information, into the core fabric of the story. Now it is time for energy, for passion, for emotion, for all of those qualities that draw you into a story and that engage you and hold your attention. The items to remember and the hint above will keep you from swerving too far afield form your original intent.

This step is akin to writers diving into the energy of a first draft. Steps 1 through 6 provide the planning needed to make this a purposeful and influential story. Now make it a captivating and engaging one as well. Don't stop to correct and to edit. Let the energy flow and get the story out and on paper.

After the story is complete, *then* worry about the precision that comes from repeated editing. If you stop to edit too soon, you will likely destroy the energy and passion that can best enter the story during that initial drafting.

■ ■ ■

STORIES TO TELL

Effective stories emerge from walking step by step through the process.

That having been said, there are a number of types (or "models") of story for you to keep in mind as you collect and organize your stories and as you place stories within your written, video, and live offerings. Remember, story models are only that—models. Consider them as suggestive ideas of what others have done and of what has worked in the past.

Here are a dozen models of stories that will, hopefully, inspire you in your use of stories. There is no particular hierarchy to this list, and there is considerable overlap between individual types. Let the various types serve to nudge your creative motors to life as you search for the stories that will best serve your exact needs. I found myself wishing as a reader that there were stories for each of these types—alas, another book I think.

1. History stories

A story by American storyteller Dan Kedding ends, "As my grandmother always said, 'It is impossible to hate once you know a person's stories.' " The goal of history stories is to make you, your organization, or your company interesting to, and trusted by, your intended audience.

A caution: Don't make your history stories *just* about your successes. Focus these stories on your goals, motives, and struggles. How did you start? How have you survived your trials and tribulations? Make sure these stories include plenty of struggle and risk and danger in order to elicit empathy and emotional involvement.

2. Who are we? stories

These are the present tense version of history stories. These are not "where did we come from" and "how did we get here" stories. They are "who are we now" and "what are we all about" stories. These stories are never fiction or even fictionalized.

Again, the caution. Don't just talk about how good you are. Rather, focus on how dedicated you are, on how noble and valuable your goals are, on the challenges you face, and on the needs you serve.

3. Concept (teaching) stories

Used almost as a narrative metaphor, concept stories make people comfortable with, and seemingly familiar with, a concept that was previously unknown (or unknowable). In the story the new concept is presented through commonly accessible analogies and likenesses that give audiences the metaphoric feeling of knowing and understanding.

Like metaphors themselves these stories can be both powerful and valuable in creating a common perspective for everyone in your audience to use when approaching your topic and material.

4. Framing stories

Framing stories open a document, video, or presentation or a series of such releases. I often open workshops with a short story whose punch line focuses on the concept of unorthodox ways to get results. That theme (what *really* creates results?) then comes up over and over during the workshop. Each time it does, it seems to create a sense of continuity and connectedness, placing the current teaching point within the context of the entire workshop.

Framing stories are used to "frame" a topic—to place it in context for further or future discussion. Framing stories are most often fictional (even cartoon like)—but certainly don't have to be. Framing stories often leave some question hanging in the air (e.g., "Is that *really* how it started?") so that the question can become the focus of subsequent activity.

Teachers often use framing stories (how the moon came to be, why the animals stopped talking, or the many origin stories, for example) to launch a new teaching unit, using the story to set a common perspective on the general subject to be studied.

5. Future vision stories

Future vision stories must create a compelling future vision, get the audience to buy into that vision, and then lay out a pathway toward it that includes you, your services, and your information. Vision stories gather support for change. They create a common goal (the future vision) in audience members.

Vision stories are a must. You have to have a strong vision story if you want to excite an audience about your programs, products, and services.

By definition, these are fiction stories. (They are about a future that hasn't happened yet.) However, they must be so vivid, compelling, and real that your audience can readily envision this future as a real and highly desirable one.

6. WOW stories

Most jobs, most professions, most activities require far more complexity, skill, care, and effort than any outside person could imagine. It is common for slight-of-hand magicians to practice hundreds of times to master even the simplest card manipulations. Many spend as much time practicing as the rest of us do working at our day job. Same with musicians . . . Wow!

From nuclear science to gardening, to accounting, to bridge painting, to high-stakes card playing, vivid stories of the *activity* may seem mundane to the people in that particular "family" but not to outsiders. It is always a Wow! moment when you realize what goes into someone else's activity or profession. Tell stories that focus on the complexity, complications, required precision, dedication, and pressures of doing what you do, and you'll give your audience a new appreciation for, and belief in, both you and what you do.

7. Struggle stories

Stories that focus on the struggles you face (and willingly accept) for a noble cause always engender empathy and support. Remember, don't focus on the outcome (your triumphs and successes) but on the struggles to get there and the motives that keep you willing to make the effort.

8. Context and relevance stories

Context and relevance stories are short, tightly focused stories that hone in on a specific problem, dilemma, or concern. In these stories we watch a real or fictional character struggle against a problem or situation that the target audience is likely to later face or confront. The story focuses on the problem and on the risk and danger it represents.

These are most often nonfiction stories (but can be very effectively created as fiction). They emphasize the scope, risk, danger, and potential consequences of a problem. They should either stop before resolution or resolve negatively for the story characters. Goal and motive are implied to be "Solve this problem!" Through the story, that goal is transferred to the audience.

9. Put-a-face-on-it stories

These are stories that make something that is abstract or merely statistical seem real, physically tangible, and personal. You present a concept with its facts and statistics and then introduce a character and that one character's story as an example of the common struggles and dilemmas of a general demographic. These stories focus on the activity of one character who becomes the "common representative" for a much larger group (one farmer, one soldier, one mayor, one homeless person, one polar bear, etc.).

Use these stories to make a quick and forceful point, and to add an emotional and personal element to a factual and statistical presentation. These stories make a presented situation, problem, action, or solution seem real, human, and personal.

Put-a-face-on-it stories are also used to highlight successes in the form of "here's how you do it" example stories. They serve as minor inspirations by showing examples of people successfully applying the thematic concepts and information. These are always nonfiction stories about real people who exemplify the behavior and attitude you want to promote. These stories always end with successes. They serve as positive role model examples and inspiration.

10. Values and beliefs stories

Value stories present events and moments that clearly and dramatically portray the core values of your organization or company. These are always nonfiction stories in which the application of some company value is critical to the outcome of the climax and resolution. They illustrate the values you work by.

Collecting these stories is a big part of the function of an organizational story culture.

11. I-am-you stories

Many organizations and companies use stories to build identity with their associates, their client base, or the population they serve. These are typically short and are based on specific experiences and incidents. The general purpose is to communicate that "we know your issues, how you think, what you need, what you value." Once you create that sense of identity and buy-in in an audience, it readily transfers from you to the information, products, and services you want to promote.

12. Ongoing stories

The idea is to break a complex topic into component, sequential parts. Create a single character and have that character face the challenges of each separate part one at a time as he or she is fed information to solve that one part. In the next episode, the character moves on to the next aspect of the complex problem. This main character is a surrogate for the target audience's attempts to master the same complex problem.

These stories are typically presented in serial form and are excellent for a series of connected, sequential lesson points or podcasts, with each episode presenting one portion of some larger and more general topic. The characters who populate the ongoing story connect the individual packets of information and individual "chapter" themes together into a unified whole.

■ ■ ■

STORY SNARES: THINGS TO AVOID

There are many narrative potholes along the road. Some are minor irritants, some just inconveniences. Some, however, are deep and sharp enough to flatten your tires and wreck the undercarriage. These are the ones to studiously avoid. Yet, each of these deadly potholes is marked by the skid marks and tire tracks of the many who have unwittingly driven straight into them.

Dodge around these gaping holes and you'll steer clear of the worst of the possible catastrophes your stories can create.

1. Bragging

I know you deserve to boast a bit. You want to highlight your successes and your triumphs. But if the audience perceives your well-earned pats on your own back as bragging, it can be catastrophic. It is always perceived as a HUGE negative.

It's not that people don't want to hear about how good you are. They do. But make your successes also the audience's successes. When you triumph, you do it for them. Keep the stories centered on the audience to create context and relevance, and your success stories will be big hits.

Don't overlook stories or anecdotes where you are the butt of the joke or about moments of your temporary failures and setbacks. They make you human and show that you can laugh at yourself, which are very alluring character traits for an audience to perceive.

2. All about *you*

Yes, your stories are technically about you, what you do, how you do it, your history, your future vision, and your information. However, remember the critical importance of **relevance**. Your audience has to think that you are telling the story for *their* benefit and are telling about you in order to help *them*. The focus must be on the audience, what's in it for them, how they'll use it, and so on.

Every reader and listener regularly bounces back to the question, "What's in here for *me*?" If they believe you just want to tell the story of you, their answer far too often will be, "Nothing," and you have lost them.

You still get to tell your story. But (step 1 of the Seven Step Story Process) you need to express that story in phraseology and vocabulary that will tap into your audience's Banks of Prior Knowledge and that will make your story relevant to them.

3. Second-person stories

Every time you say, "You come into our showroom and you will be dazzled by . . ." a significant portion of your audience will say, "No, I won't." And you have lost them for the rest of your talk, or of your paper.

It can be quite effective to tell your stories in second person—it *can be*. But be forewarned. There is a great risk. Anytime a person rejects your second-person statements ("I wouldn't do that . . . or think that . . . or feel that!"), you have lost that person. Unless your second-person story is carefully researched and crafted, it won't take long to lose much of your audience.

4. Jargon (and other "family speak")

This is just a reminder of the dangers of family stories. Use the "weekend talk" test to see if too much jargon creeps into the wording you plan to use. If you wouldn't tell it that way to neighbors over the backyard fence during a weekend barbecue, don't do it when you write or talk outside of the close-knit work family.

5. Tell, don't show

One of the most fundamental maxims of storytelling is "Show, don't tell"—and for valid reason. Rather than talking at your audience—telling them what to do or feel—share the story so that it unfolds naturally and your audience is allowed to come to their own conclusion. Giving them something to figure out and to envision on their own increases engagement. That way people don't just absorb facts and information. They actively listen to stories and make their own inferences.

When you're sharing a story, provide the sensory details that will let your audience envision the setting, the characters, and the action, and really feel the conflict and the risk and danger. Describe what's happening as if you were describing events happening right now in front of you.

6. Exaggerations (and other "fudges" on the truth)

If you claim that a story is true—even if you *imply* it is true without actually saying so—even if you are sufficiently vague so that *others* imply it—it had better be authentic and true. A faked story always begs for a monumental backlash. The cost always far exceeds the benefit. Horror story examples abound.

7. Impersonal messaging

It doesn't matter if your organization sells razors, builds cloud infrastructure, supports education research, or manages tax collection, human beings are still driving the action. Personalize the central characters of your story. Make them seem real enough so that the audience feels a stake in (and wants to know) what happens to them next. People connect with other people, so make sure you focus on the real-life characters in your story. Put a face on it!

■ ■ ■

──── *A FINAL THOUGHT* ────

I'll use this final section to place *Story Smart* into a wider perspective, to anchor it within the context of the totality of your communications needs and processes. To do that, I'll remind you of what we have covered in these pages—and of what we haven't covered.

There are two halves to the word "storytelling. "Story" is a noun, a physical "thing." "Telling," is a verb, an interactive aspect of communication. Though highly interdependent, those two halves are separate processes and involve different sets of planning and development tools, paths, and concerns.

This book has focused on the *story* half of storytelling. I have presented the most current research and information about the design and use of your stories to accomplish your goals. I have led you to the point of creating powerful, effective, influential stories worth sharing.

Consideration of the media of communication you use to *tell* your story is a separate topic—one we have not covered in this book. First, you need to have a rock-solid, effective story. Then (and only then) you can adjust the story to fit with the media you choose. Yes, you will (and must) adjust your story to accommodate the media of communication you select. Will you tell your story during live presentations or internal meetings? As part of a memo? A blog? An article? On your web site? As an ad campaign? Will it go out as a video posting? But that discussion is a topic for another day and another book following another round or two of research.

Story, the *noun*, is a powerful and versatile servant. But "story" is not your content, information, or messaging. Think of your content as the payload, worthless while it sits encased in its nosecone at your feet. Story is the delivery and guidance system that reliably propels your content to your distant target: the conscious mind and memory of your target audience. Story is the framework onto which you hang your content. Story is an approach and guide to effective communications planning. It is the way you structure, organize, and present your material.

Story Smart has concentrated on the tools, concepts, and techniques for that planning process. You know what you want to say. However, the critical question is how will your audience hear (understand and make sense of) what you say? *Story Smart* has led you through the steps to backtrack from what you want them to hear and remember to what you need to say (or write) in order to make that happen.

This reverse engineering process has relied heavily on recent neural science findings—centered on the informational needs of the human Neural Story Net. Those needed informational elements are fixed, based on the neural wiring and programming of the net. That doesn't mean that the stories you create and use must be similarly constrained and *fixed*. Just because the science of story produces fixed relationships we can even express as algebraic formulas doesn't mean that the way you choose to account for those fixed story mandates is mechanistic, rote, formulaic, or *fixed*.

Stories are infinitely malleable, flexible, and customizable entities. There is near infinite variety in how you choose to present your material while you still account for the essential elements of effective story structure. This book (in conjunction with *Story Proof: The Science Behind the Startling Power of Story*) presents the emerging science of story. Think of story science not as a constraining limit on your expression but as a tested set of powerful guideposts to keep you on a productive path toward effective stories.

You are fully in possession of the tools, concepts, and techniques you need in order to sculpt, craft, and adjust your stories to accomplish your specific purposes.

Go out and do it . . . and enjoy!

■ ■ ■

REFERENCES

Anderson, J. *Rules of the Mind.* Hillsdale, NJ: Erlbaum, 1993.

Anderson, J., and P. Martin. "Narratives and Healing: Exploring One Family's Stories of Cancer Survivorship." *Health Communications,* 15 (2003): 133–143.

Applebee, A. *The Child's Concept of Story.* Chicago: University of Chicago Press, 1978.

Azziz, R. *The Critical Art of Storytelling.* Athens, Georgia: University of Georgia Press, April 15, 2013.

Baker, Bill. *Four Facets of Strategic Storytelling.* London: Marketing Profs, May 16, 2011.

Bransford, J., and A. Brown, eds. *How People Learn.* Washington, DC: National Academy Press, 2000.

Bransford, J., and B. Stein. *The Ideal Problem Solver,* 2nd ed. New York: Freeman, 1993.

Brooks, David. *The Social Animal.* New York: Random House, 2012.

Bruner, J. *Making Stories: Law, Literature, Life.* Cambridge, MA: Harvard University Press, 2003.

Carroll, John. "Storytelling as a Casual Art." *San Francisco Chronicle,* December 7, 2012. Available at http://www.sfgate.com/entertainment/carroll/article/Storytelling-as a -casual-art-4098298.php#ixzz2FPG6xLiO

Clough, M. P. "The Story behind the Science: Bringing Science and Scientists to Life in Post-Secondary Science Education." *Science & Education,* 20, no. 7-8 (2011): 701–717.

Crick, F., and C. Koch. "Are We Aware of Neural Activity in the Primary Visual Cortex?" *Nature,* 375 (1995): 121–123.

Cron, Lisa. *Wired for Story: The Writer's Guide to Using Brain Science to Hook Readers from the Very First Sentence.* Los Angeles, UCLA Press, 2012.

Crossley, M. *Introducing Narrative Psychology.* London: Open University Press, 2000.

Crowley, T. "17 Storytelling Tips for Startups," Blog post, March 25, 2013. www.rude baguette.com

Damasio, A. *Descartes' Error: Emotion, Reason, and the Human Brain.* New York: G. Putnam's Sons, 1994.

Damasio, A. *Self Comes to Mind: Constructing the Conscious Brain.* New York: Pantheon, 2010.

Donald, M. *Origins of the Modern Mind.* Cambridge, MA: Harvard University Press, 1991.

Edleman, G. *Second Nature: Brain Science and Human Knowledge.* New Haven, CT: Yale University Press, 2006.

Edleman, G., and G. Tononi. "Reentry and the Dynamic Core: Neural Correlates of Conscious Experience." In Thomas Metzinger, ed., *Neural Correlates of Consciousness: Empirical and Conceptual Questions* (pp. 121–138). Cambridge, MA: MIT Press, 2000.

Egan, K. *Children's Minds: Talking Rabbits and Clockwork Oranges*. New York: Teachers College Press, 1999.

Farmer, Katherine. *Cracking the Story Code: A Multi-Perspective and Semiotic Approach to Script and Text Analysis*. 2015.

Firth, Chris. *Making Up the Mind: How the Brain Creates Our Mental World*. New York: Wiley-Blackwell, 2007.

Fisher, W. "Narrative as a Human Communications Paradigm: The Case of Public Moral Argument." *Communications Monograph*, 51 (1994): 1–20.

Furiga, Paul. "The Science That Proves the Effectiveness of Storytelling in Business." WordWrite Storytelling Blog, April 16, 2013. http://www.haloandnoose.com

Gottschall, Jonathan. *The Storytelling Animal: How Stories Make Us Human*. Boston: Houghton Mifflin, 2012.

Haven, K., "Section III, Appendices 1 through 5." In Y. Levchuk, C. Berka, K. Haven, and A. Kruse, *The Boeing Narrative Networks (N2) Phase I Final Report*. Arlington, VA: DARPA, 2013.

Haven, K. *Story Proof: The Science behind the Startling Power of Story*. Westport, CT: Libraries Unlimited, 2009.

Horgan, John. "The Myth of Mind Control." *Discover*, October 2004, pp. 40–46.

Hsu, J. "The Secrets of Storytelling: Our Love of Telling Tales Reveals the Working of the Mind." *Scientific American*, 19, no. 4 (August/September 2008): 48–51.

Kahneman, Daniel. *Thinking, Fast and Slow*. New York: Farrar, Straus and Giroux, 2011.

Klassen, S. "The Construction and Analysis of a Science Story: A Proposed Methodology." *Science & Education*, 18, no. 3–4 (2009): 401–423.

Konrath, Sara, et al. "Changes in Dispositional Empathy in American College Students Over Time: A Meta-Analysis." *Personality and Social Psychology Review*. May 2011, vol. 15, no. 2, 180–198.

Kotulak, R. *Inside the Brain: Revolutionary Discoveries of How the Mind Works*. Kansas City, MO: Andrews McNeal, 1999.

Kotulak, R. *The Learning Revolution*. Kansas City, MO: Andrews McNeal, 2005.

Kruglinski, S. "Big Blue to Build a Brain." *Discover*, September 2005, p. 9.

Lakoff, G., and M. Johnson. *Metaphors We Live By*. Chicago: University of Chicago Press, 2003.

Lakoff, G., and M. Johnson. *Philosophy in the Flesh: The Embodied Mind and Its Challenge to Western Thought*. New York: Basic Books, 1999.

Montague, R. *Why Choose This Book?: How We Make Decisions*. New York: Dutton, 2006.

Nelson, K. "Narratives and the Emergence of a Consciousness of Self." In G. Fireman et al., eds., *Narrative and Consciousness: Literature, Psychology and the Brain* (pp. 17–36). New York: Oxford University Press, 2003.

Newman, M. "The Importance of Storytelling as a Tool in the Practice of Law." *Legal Intelligencer*, April 19, 2013, pp. 147–153.

Newquist, H. *The Great Brain Book*. New York: Scholastic Reference, 2004.

Nyhan, Brendon et al. "Effective Messages in Vaccine Promotion: A Randomized Trial." Dartmouth College, 2014. doi: 10.1542/peds.2013-2365.

Paul, Annie. "Your Brain on Fiction." *New York Times*, March 17, 2012.

Pennebaker, James W. *The Secret Life of Pronouns: What Our Words Say about Us*. New York: Bloomsberry, 2011.

Pinker, S. *How the Mind Works*. New York: W. W. Norton, 1997.

Pinker, S. *The Language Instinct*. New York: Perennial Classic, 2000.

Plotkin, H., ed. *Learning, Development, and Culture: Essays in Evolutionary Espitemology*. New York: Wiley, 1982.

PsysOrg.com. "Readers Build Vivid Mental Simulations of Narrative Situations, Brain Scans Suggest," January 6, 2009, http://www.phyorg.com/print152210728.html

Ramachandran, V. S. *The Tell-Tale Brain*. New York: W.W. Norton, 2011.

Ramachandran, V. S. *A Brief Tour of Human Consciousness*. New York: Pi Press, 2004.

Rose, Frank. *The Art of Immersion*. New York: W.W. Norton, 2011.

Sachs, Jonas. *Winning the Story Wars*. Cambridge, MA: Harvard Business Review Press, 2012.

Schank, R. "Every Curriculum Tells a Story." *Tech Directions*, 62, no. 2 (2000): 25–29.

Schank, R. *Tell Me a Story*. New York: Charles Scribner's Sons, 1990.

Scheffer, Victor. *The Year of the Whale*. New York: Charles Scribner's Sons, 1969.

Signorelli, Jim. *Story Branding: Creating Standout Brands through the Power of Story*. Austin, TX: Greenleaf, 2012.

Silverman, L. *Wake Me Up when the Data Is Over: How Organizations Use Storytelling to Drive Results*. Jonesborough, TN: National Storytelling Network, 2006.

Simmons, A. *The Story Factor*. New York: Basic Books, 2001.

Smith, Derek. "What 17 Industry Leaders Think about Digital Storytelling." *Huffington Post*, April 22, 2013.

Taylor, D. *The Healing Power of Stories*. New York: Doubleday, 1996.

Tomasello, M. "Understanding the Self as Social Agent." In P. Rochat, ed., *The Self in Infancy: Theory and Research* (pp. 449–460). Amsterdam: Elsevier, 1995.

Turner, M. *The Literary Mind: The Origins of Thought and Language*. New York: Oxford University Press, 1996.

Widrich, L. "The Science of Storytelling." BufferBlog.com, February 21, 2013.

Widrich, L. "The Science of Storytelling: Why Telling a Story Is the Most Powerful Way to Activate Our Brains." BufferBlog.com, December 5, 2012.

Willingham, D. Daniel Willingham: Science and Education Blog, dtwuva@gmail.com, June 3, 2013.

Wolf, Maryanne. *Proust and the Squid: The Story and Science of the Reading Brain*. New York: Harper Perennial, 2007.

Zak, Paul. *The Moral Molecule*. New York: Dutton, 2012.

INDEX

About the Author

KENDALL HAVEN is the only internationally recognized expert in the science of story structure. He was the only storyteller to participate in the Defense Advanced Research Projects Agency (DARPA) Narrative Networks project to research the neural and cognitive science of how stories exert influence. Previously Haven spent eight years as a senior research scientist for the Department of Energy. His published works include 24 books from Libraries Unlimited, including *Story Proof: The Science behind the Startling Power of Story*; *Crash Course in Storytelling*; and *Super Simple Storytelling: A Can-Do Guide for Every Classroom, Every Day.*

33826095R00104

Made in the USA
Middletown, DE
18 January 2019